Journey to English 4

CARINA GUINAME SHIROMA
MAURICIO SHIROMA

MACMILLAN

MACMILLAN

Executive managing editor: Wilma Moura
Editors: Andréa Vidal and Isabel Lacombe
Assistant editor: Ana Carolina de Castro Gasonato
Language consultant: Robert C. Garner
Teacher's guide collaborator: Vitor Sugita
Proofreader: Maria Cecilia Jorgewich Skaf
Translators: Amini Rassoul, Anthony Doyle, and Maria Cecilia Jorgewich Skaf
Permissions coordinator: Fernando Santos
Minidictionary editor: Ana Carolina de Castro Gasonato

Concept design and page make-up by : Maps World Produções Gráficas
Design editor: Jorge Okura
Cover concept and design: Alexandre Tallarico
Concept design: Alexandre Tallarico and Carolina de Oliveira
Page make-up: Alexandre Tallarico, Carolina de Oliveira, and Vivian Trevizan
Proofreader: Ana Cristina Mendes Perfetti

Illustrator: Sidney Meireles (Giz de Cera)

Audio recording, mixing, and mastering: Maximal Studio
DVD illustrations, animations, infographs, software, and website: Maximal Studio

Dados Internacionais de Catalogação na Publicação (CIP)
(Câmara Brasileira do Livro, SP, Brasil)

Shiroma, Carina Guiname
Journey to English / Carina Guiname Shiroma, Mauricio Shiroma. -- 1. ed. -- São Paulo : Macmillan, 2012.

Manual do professor.
ISBN 978-85-7418-863-8 (v. 1, inglês)
ISBN 978-85-7418-870-6 (v. 1, português)
ISBN 978-85-7418-865-2 (v. 2, inglês)
ISBN 978-85-7418-871-3 (v. 2, português)
ISBN 978-85-7418-867-6 (v. 3, inglês)
ISBN 978-85-7418-872-0 (v. 3, português)
ISBN 978-85-7418-869-0 (v. 4, inglês)
ISBN 978-85-7418-873-7 (v. 4, português)

1. Inglês (Ensino fundamental) I. Shiroma, Mauricio. II. Título.

12-06866 CDD-372.652

Índices para catálogo sistemático:
1. Inglês : Ensino fundamental 372.652

Macmillan do Brasil
Rua José Félix de Oliveira, 383 – Granja Viana
06708-645 – Cotia – SP – Brasil
www.macmillan.com.br
elt@macmillan.com.br

Impresso no Brasil - Corprint - Janeiro/2015

Caro aluno,

Você já deve ter ouvido que "toda jornada começa com o primeiro passo", não é? Pois o primeiro passo da nossa jornada foi dado há muito tempo, quando nós tínhamos a sua idade e começamos a estudar inglês.

Quando embarcamos nessa viagem que é aprender uma nova língua, tínhamos os sonhos de todos os viajantes: visitar lugares distantes, conhecer pessoas incríveis, entender o que o mundo fala e conseguir nos comunicar com ele. Porém, naquela época, antes das maravilhas e facilidades tecnológicas que você conhece hoje, a jornada era bastante difícil: havia muitos obstáculos e poucos atalhos. As dificuldades deixavam a jornada mais lenta, mas nem por isso menos interessante.

O segredo de todo bom viajante é saber se adaptar ao ritmo que cada trecho impõe. Em alguns trechos, viajamos na velocidade da luz; em outros, nos deixamos levar pela maré calma. Além disso, como em toda jornada, havia muitos caminhos à frente, e saber escolher o melhor deles fazia parte do desafio de chegar. Apesar de o destino ter sido o objetivo final da jornada, saber aproveitar as delícias do percurso foi, sem dúvida, o que mais nos encantou.

"Mas eles chegaram aonde?", você deve estar se perguntando.

Chegamos aqui, agora. E já podemos traçar o caminho para você, que está dando aquele primeiro passo rumo à mesma jornada de aprender uma língua.

Este livro é um mapa da jornada para você; use-o, transforme-o, descubra novos caminhos e possibilidades. Compartilhe as experiências com outros viajantes e divirta-se sempre.

Que você faça uma excelente viagem!

Carina e Mauricio

Know your book

Unit sections

Opening
The pictures in the opening pages of each unit are intended to stimulate impressions, feelings, and reactions, and lead to reflection on the theme.

Itinerary
Itinerary introduces the contents explored in each unit. This section allows you to evaluate what you already know and get ready / prepare yourself for what you will learn.

INFER

This icon indicates that the question(s) can only be answered by using logical deduction along with the information in the text.

Your Take
In these activities, you give your opinion and share ideas with classmates about the topics explored in the unit.

Reading
In the reading activities, you analyze and interpret different texts and learn strategies to make reading easier and more enjoyable. This section provides not only basic reading comprehension tasks, but also topics for reflection and discussion which will contribute to your education as a critical citizen.

GENRE

This icon indicates activities that focus on the characteristics of the text genre studied.

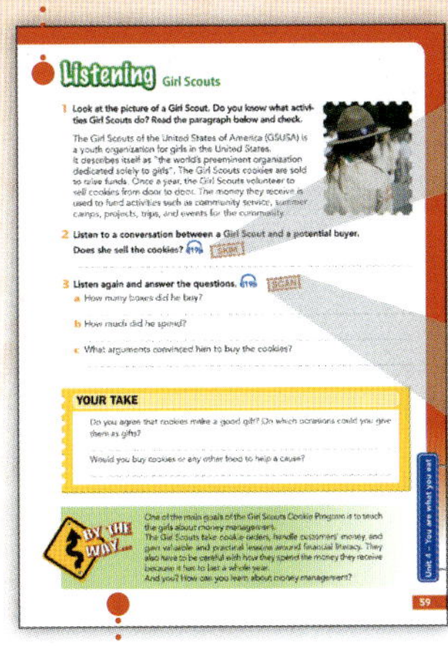

Listening

In this section, you listen to a great variety of oral genres. The activities use strategies that make listening easier.

SKIM This icon indicates that the activity provides practice for understanding the gist of the text.

SCAN This icon indicates that the activity practices comprehension of specific and detailed information from the text.

By the Way

This section provides comments about language and culture to expand and contextualize the different topics in the unit.

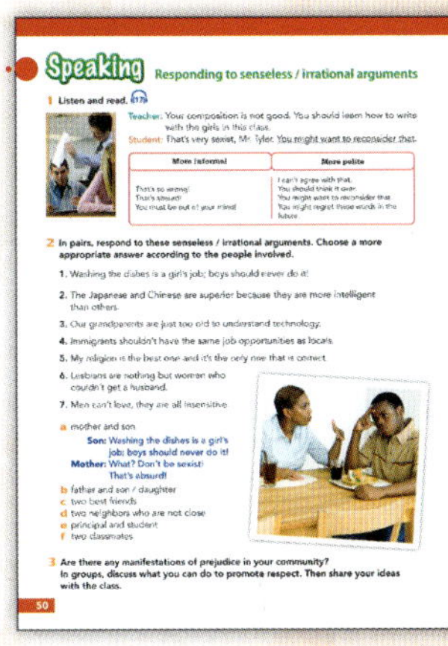

Speaking

In this section you learn how to gradually communicate in English in daily situations through conversation activities – from the most simple, such as making suggestions, to the most complex, such as making a speech in class.

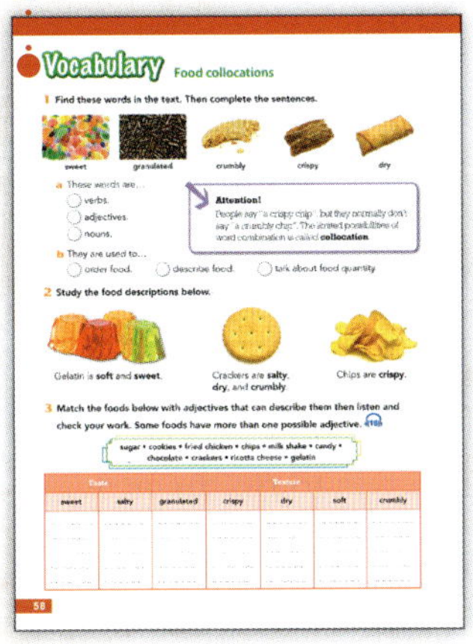

Vocabulary

In this section, you learn the meaning and pronunciation of words and expressions, which will expand your possibilities of communication in English. The section also helps you organize your knowledge.

Pronunciation

Pronunciation works as a support for the speaking and oral comprehension activities. This section contains dialogs, visual aids, and phonetic symbols to make you feel more confident and become more efficient in oral communication.

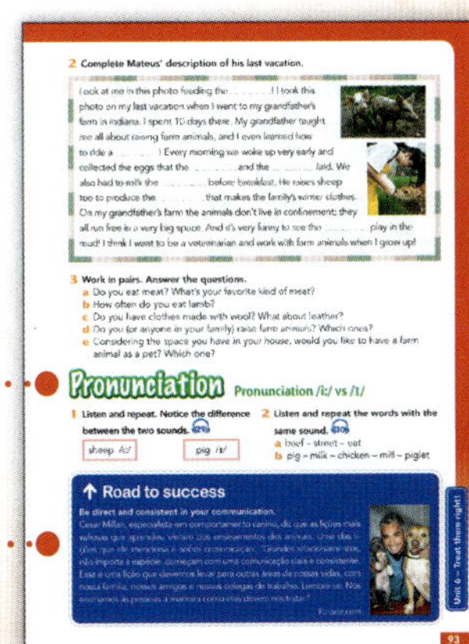

Grammar

In this section, you are exposed to grammar within a communicative context to facilitate understanding. The activities help you analyze the patterns of language and draw conclusions about its rules. With this material, you learn how to use grammar both to produce and to understand oral and written texts.

Road to Success

This section helps develop learner autonomy in general by providing several strategies, techniques, and tips for you to succeed in learning English.

Writing

Writing is seen as a process. Here you learn to use different resources to plan, outline, revise, and edit so you can write with autonomy. The genres you will produce will be shared with different audiences and published in different media.

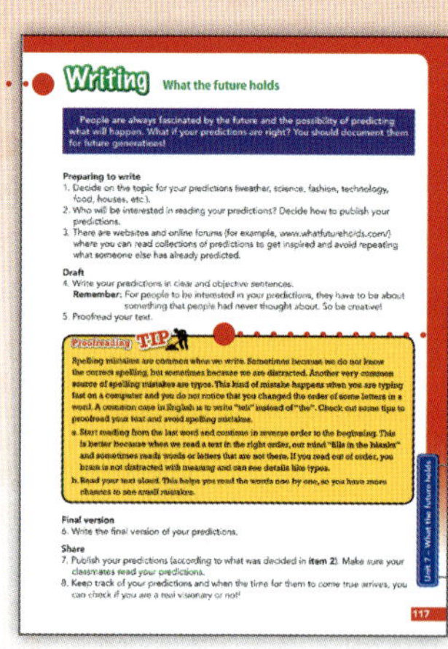

Proofreading Tip

These boxes provide practical production, revision, and editing tips for you to gradually achieve autonomy in the writing process.

Crossroads

Here you use English to learn, expand, or review contents from other school subjects.

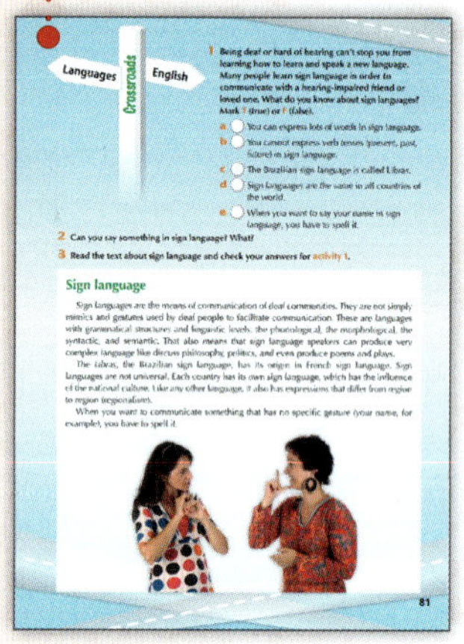

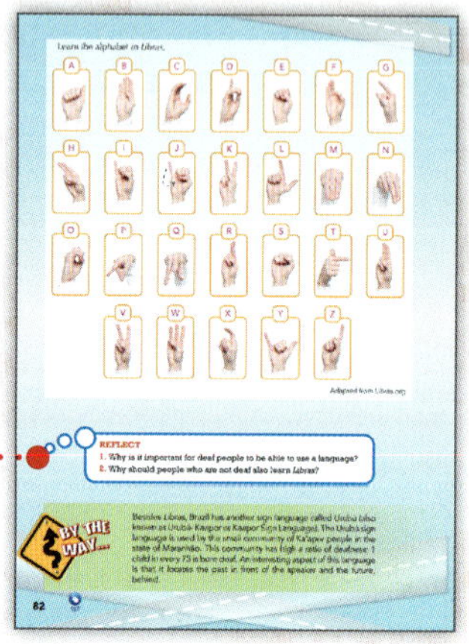

Reflect

In this section, you think over the activities and texts in order to develop a critical sense. It encourages your personal engagement as a citizen.

This icon tells you that there is an activity on the DVD-ROM. When you see this symbol, go to page 166 and find the objectives, description, and tips to do the activity.

Extras

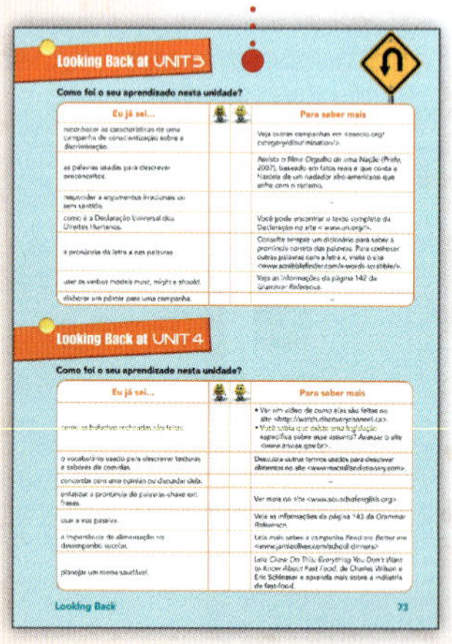

Looking Back

At the end of each unit, this self-evaluation tool will help you develop autonomy in learning English. Here you reflect on whether you have reached the goals established or still need more revision. You will also find suggestions for further study, such as websites, other resources in this book, and other useful titles.

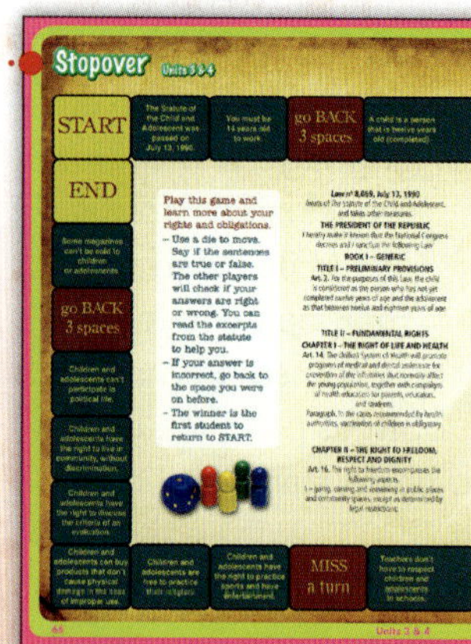

Stopover

Every two units, you stop to review the content with fun and relaxing activities. This section will allow you to evaluate yourself and improve your knowledge in an enjoyable way.

Review

Every four units, you have a systematic, comprehensive review. You can test your knowledge and judge whether you need to practice more or not.

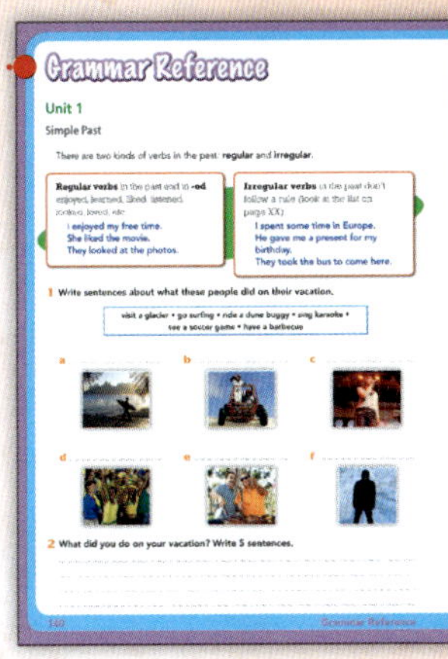

Grammar Reference

All the knowledge built in class is systematized in this section. It works as reference to study and review grammar.

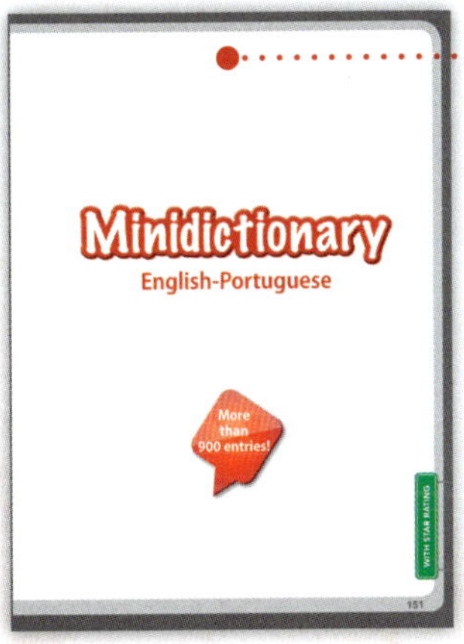

Minidictionary

This is a bilingual dictionary with all the key words introduced in each book. Organized in alphabetical order, it provides the translation of the word or expression, the phonetic transcription, the word frequency, the word class, and examples of use.

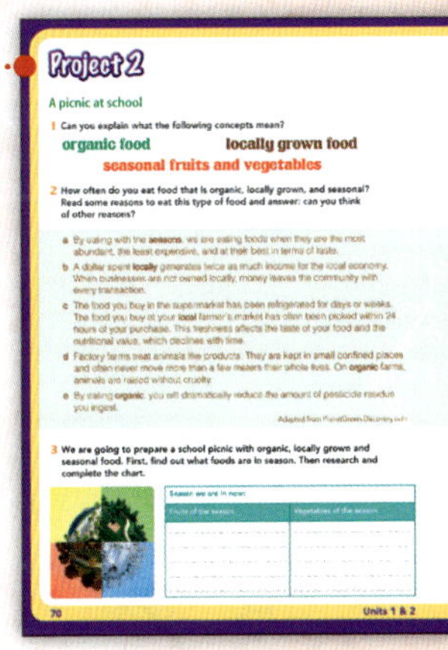

Project

Every two units there is a project involving research, planning, preparation, and presentation. It is an opportunity to put English into practice in real contexts both inside and outside of school.

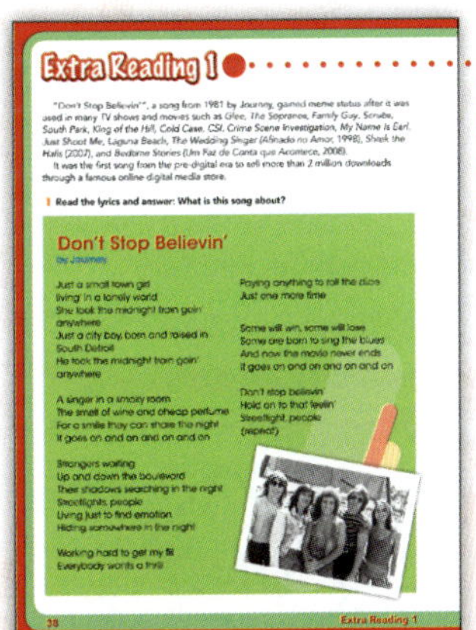

Extra Reading

Every two units, there is an extra text to develop reading skills. The texts are authentic and accompanied by activities that provide more practice for you to feel comfortable when reading.

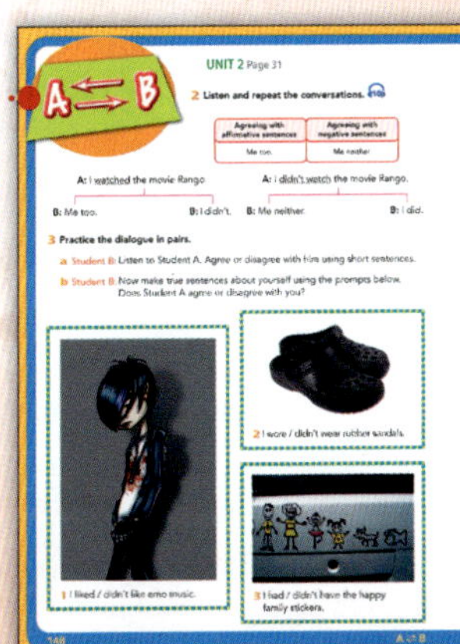

A ⇄ B

For some conversation practices, there are special activities that can only be done with the exchange of information between two students. The section simulates a situation that is common in our daily speech – the search for information.

Contents

UNIT 1

UNIT 2

UNIT 3

UNIT 4

Name: ....

School: ....

School address: ....

....

City: ....

State: ....

ZIP code: ....

School telephone number: ....

School email: ....

English teacher: ....

Class schedule

Monday	Tuesday	Wednesday	Thursday	Friday	Saturday

Test agenda

January	February	March	April	May	June
July	August	September	October	November	December

Classroom Language

UNIT 1

Give me a break!

ITINERARY

In this unit, you will develop the following competences:

- reading a review to get more information about a hotel;
- learning words to talk about free time activities;
- reflecting on how you can use your leisure time to learn English;
- using the Simple Past and the correct pronunciation of verbs in the past to talk about a vacation;
- giving opinions to talk about past events;
- reading about vacations in the Northern Hemisphere to learn more about the seasons;
- listening to a testimonial to get general and specific information and infer about spending vacations at a summer camp;
- writing a review to evaluate a place.

Reading A hotel review

1 **A review is an opinion about something, a critical analysis of a film, book, song, exhibition, restaurant, hotel, equipment, etc. for public audiences. It usually appears in newspapers, magazines, and on specialized websites. What do you know about a review? Match the information to the categories below.** GENRE

a what the person who reads a review wants

b what is included in the language of a review

c the objectives of a review

( )
- adjectives to describe the product / service or how the writer feels about it
- sentences in the first person

( )
- complain about something
- recommend something or not
- advertise something

( )
- know more about something before buying, using, or paying for it
- agree or disagree with the writer's opinion
- know more about something after buying, using, or paying for it

2 **Match.**

a pool

b water slides

c arcade

d staff

e room

( ) 

( ) 

( ) 

( ) 

( ) 

3 **Read these three reviews about the same hotel and answer: would you stay there? Why? Why not?**

....

....

....

....

tripadvisor®

CanadianTraveler883
Toronto

Reviewer
3 reviews

"A Kid's Paradise"

Reviewed December 20, 2010.

I'm a single dad and I took my 8-year-old son. I showed him the pictures on the website, and he simply couldn't wait. He was not disappointed at all!! He loved the pool, water slides, facilities (e.g. arcade) and wanted to use the pool up to the very last minute of check in. The rooms were very nice, and everything was clean. If you're a family with kids of 10 or less, this is THE PLACE! The staff was very friendly and helpful as well.

more ▼

Was this review helpful? Yes

Problem with this review?

Traci3573
Tampa, Florida

Reviewer
2 reviews

"Best Spring Break EVER!!!!!"

Reviewed May 12, 2011.

This hotel is more than just a hotel. It is a character / water theme park. You check in and you don't have to go anywhere to have a good time. Everything you need is right there. Our kids absolutely loved it. The staff was more than hospitable. They made you feel like an old friend, even a family member. This is definitely our new vacation spot!

more ▼

Was this review helpful? Yes

Problem with this review?

Gregatebay
Denver

Reviewer
2 reviews

"Very disappointing. Expensive and very low quality"

Reviewed August 22, 2011.

We stayed with our 3 children between 5 and 9. It was very disappointing. Pools had smelly water and were extremely crowded. Rooms were very small. Food was very poor quality – like a cafeteria. Advertised "in room video games" meant you had to pay $5 per game / day. I would definitely not stay there again.

more ▼

Was this review helpful? Yes

Problem with this review?

Adapted from TripAdvisor.com

4 Read again and answer. SCAN

a Who chose the hotel after checking it out on the Internet?

....

b Who doesn't mention any facilities (pool, arcade, etc.)?

....

c Does Gregatebay complain about the hotel staff?

....

d Do Gregatebay's children complain about the hotel?

....

e Does Traci3573 have more than one child?

....

YOUR TAKE

Why should you complain about services and products when you are not satisfied with them?

....

....

....

Vocabulary Free time activities

1 Match the words with the correct picture.

a horse
b snorkeling
c beach
d karaoke
e hiking
f hang out
g mall

2 Use the words below to form free time activities with the verbs on the next page. Then listen to check your work. 3

hiking	to the beach
the Internet	home
karaoke	shopping
a bike	a picnic
at the mall	snorkeling
with friends	at the pool
a horse	

Go to the beach.

1 Surf ....

2 Hang out ....

3 Sing ....

4 Stay ....

5 Go ....

6 Ride ....

7 Swim ....

8 Have ....

3 Answer.

a What is your favorite vacation activity?

....

b What is a good place to hang out with friends in your city?

....

c How often do you surf the Internet?

....

d Which activities (listed on this page) would you like to try?

....

e What is your least favorite vacation activity?

....

↑ Road to success

Leisure time, learning time

Você pode aproveitar seu tempo livre para se divertir e, ao mesmo tempo, aprender inglês:

- Assista novamente a filmes que você já viu, mas sem legendas e com o som original, tentando se lembrar dos diálogos entre os personagens.
- Leia, traduza, memorize e cante as suas músicas favoritas.
- Evite ver programas de TV e filmes dublados; prefira os legendados. Uma opção é usar o recurso SAP (canal de áudio original) que muitas redes de TV oferecem como opção para programas de TV dublados.
- Com a ajuda de um dicionário, traduza as telas de menus, os vídeos de introdução e os comandos de *videogame* que você não conhece.
- Em museus, leia também a versão em inglês dos textos explicativos das obras expostas.

Grammar
Simple Past (I)

1 Read the dialog and answer the questions.

Leonardo: What **did** you **do** on your vacation?
Marcelo: **I traveled** to João Pessoa, and **my family stayed** at home. And you?
Leonardo: **I went** to my aunt's house in the countryside, and after that **my cousins came** here to stay with me for a few days. **We had** a great time.
Marcelo: **I saw** lots of interesting things in João Pessoa. Oh, and **I ate** crabs when **I visited** Solon de Lucena Park!

a The verbs in the past are the same for *I, you, he, she, it, we, they.*
◯ true ◯ false

b All the verbs in the past end in *-ed.*
◯ true ◯ false

c In questions we use…
◯ *did* + verb in the infinitive.
◯ *did* + verb in the past.

d In affirmative sentences we use…
◯ *did* + verb in the past.
◯ the verb in the past.

2 The verbs *travel*, *stay*, and *visit* are examples of regular verbs (that always end in *-ed*). Find more examples of regular verbs in the reviews on page 15.

....

3 The verbs *go*, *come*, *have*, *see*, and *eat* are examples of irregular verbs (that have different forms). Find more examples of irregular verbs in the reviews on page 15.

....

4 **Look at the table of verbs at the end of your book and find out if the verbs in the box are regular or irregular. Write them in the table below.**

~~buy~~ • ~~dance~~ • drink • enjoy • get • give • hear • know • learn • like • listen • look • love • read • speak • take • talk • think • walk • want • do • spend • sleep • watch • show • make • mean

Regular		Irregular	
Infinitive	Past	Infinitive	Past
dance	danced	buy	bought

5 **Complete the dialog with verbs in the past.**

Lucas: What did you do on your vacation, Claudia?

Claudia: I .... a lot. 12 hours a day! And you?

Lucas: Me too. And I .... some time with my friends online and on the street. I .... you were at your grandma's in Fortaleza.

Claudia: Not this year. I just .... a lot of TV and .... 3 books at home.

Lucas: It was a little boring. I .... to travel or go to the movies.

Claudia: Yeah, I know. I .... to my school friends yesterday, and they .... their vacations were not very exciting.

6 **Work in pairs. Ask your partner these questions.**

a What did you drink this morning?
b Who did you see this morning?
c When did you speak to your best friend?
d Where did you go last Saturday?

Pronunciation The *-ed* sound

1 Listen to the *-ed* sounds in these verbs. Are they the same? (4)

wanted – stopped – listened

....

....

2 Listen again and answer. Which *-ed* sounds more like... (4)

/ɪd/ ? ....

/d/ ? ....

/t/ ? ....

3 Study the rules. Then listen and repeat the verbs. (5)

For verbs ending with the **sounds** /d/ and /t/, the final ***-ed*** is pronounced /ɪd/.	For verbs ending with the **sounds** /p/, /k/, /f/, /s/, /ʃ/ and /tʃ/, the final ***-ed*** is pronounced /t/. The letter ***e*** is not pronounced.	For verbs with different endings, the final ***-ed*** is pronounced /d/. The letter ***e*** is not pronounced.
en**d**ed wan**t**ed	lau**gh**ed dan**c**ed	liste**n**ed pla**y**ed

a /ɪd/ graded – decided – exited – directed – objected
b /t/ washed – watched – faxed – liked – missed – helped – stuffed
c /d/ tried – saved – pleased – enjoyed – called – explained

Speaking Opinions about past events

1 Listen to the conversation. (6)

Carly: How was your weekend, Jasmin?
Jasmin: It was OK. I stayed at home and read a book. What did you do last weekend?
Carly: We went to my grandma's house in the countryside.
Jasmin: Oh, really? How did you like it?
Carly: It was nice. My grandma is an excellent cook, and there's a swimming pool there.

2 Talk to three classmates about the weekend.

166

Geography | Crossroads | English

1 **Why do you think the longest vacation period in school happens in summer?**

2 **Read the text and answer T (true) or F (false).**

Summer vacations

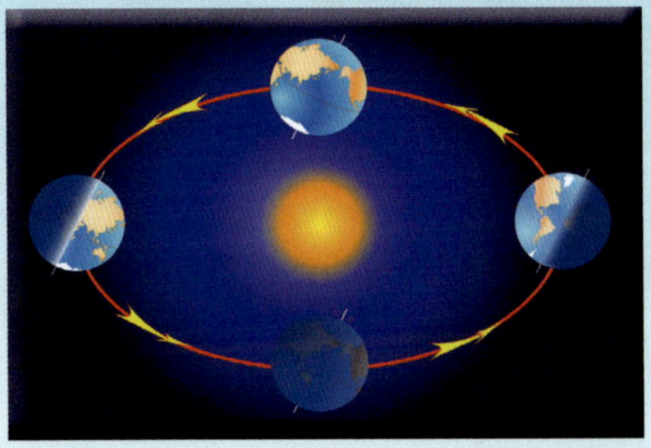

In most countries, the longest school break coincides with summertime and it lasts about 5 or 8 weeks. For countries in the Northern Hemisphere (the part of the planet that is north of the equator), like the United States for example, summer vacation is normally from the end of May to the end of August or the end of June to early September, depending on the state. For countries in the Southern Hemisphere, like Brazil, it is normally from early December to early-February.

But when it is summer in the USA, it is winter in Brazil. Why is that so? The different seasons are the result of the tilt (inclination) of the Earth's axis in relation to the Sun.

The different quantity of sunlight on the Earth during the year defines the four seasons of the year – spring, summer, autumn (or fall), and winter.

Summer is hotter than winter because the light of the Sun hits the Earth at a more direct angle during summer than during winter. And as the Earth moves around the Sun during the year, different parts of it are hit, more or less directly.

Adapted from InfoPlease.com

a The equator divides the planet into Northern and Southern hemispheres. ◯

b The Earth is closer to the Sun in summer. ◯

c The quantity of sunlight determines the temperature on the planet. ◯

3 **Complete the chart below with the months for each season in your country.**

	Northern Hemisphere	Southern Hemisphere
Winter	December, January, February	....
Spring	March, April, May	....
Summer	June, July, August	....
Autumn (Fall)	September, October, November	....

BY THE WAY...

The temperature doesn't change because the Earth is closer to the Sun in summer and farther in winter. Actually, the Earth is farthest from the Sun in July and is closest to the Sun in January.

166

Listening A testimonial

GENRE

A **testimonial** is a recommendation of the quality of a product or service.

1 Read the text below and listen to Antoine's testimonial. Do you feel like going to summer camp after listening to his recommendation? Why (not)? 7 SKIM

Antoine gave a testimonial of his experience at Green Pack Summer Camp to be posted on their website. A *summer camp* is a program for children or teenagers (known as *campers*) that is normally offered during summer, with recreational and sports activities supervised by a counselor.

2 Listen again and answer. 7 SCAN

a How old is he? ....

b Is this his first time at a summer camp? ....

c Was his first time a good experience? ....

d What was NOT mentioned by Antoine?

- ◯ He made new friends.
- ◯ He learned a lot of skills.
- ◯ The counselors were very strict.
- ◯ He had new experiences.
- ◯ He learned about himself.
- ◯ You can do lots of things that you can't normally do at home.

YOUR TAKE

Can you imagine some advantages and disadvantages of spending your vacation at a summer camp?

....

....

3 What is similar between a testimonial and a review? And what is different? INFER

....

....

4 What feelings does Antoine express in the audio?

....

....

5 How important is this change in mood for the message? Why?

....

....

Writing A review

There are many websites specialized in helping travelers and visitors choose the best vacation experience. Most of these websites count on contributions of the people who visited the places and have an opinion to share.

Preparing to write

1. Think about a place you visited. Is it a hotel, a restaurant, or an attraction? What's its name?
2. Was your experience there mostly positive or negative? How would you rate the place: 5-star (excellent), 4-star (very good), 3-star (average), 2-star (poor), or 1-star (terrible)?

Draft

3. Write your review. Write your general opinion, mention details, and justify your impressions by giving examples.
4. Give your review a title.
5. Proofread your text.

Remember: Your title has to summarize the ideas of the review.

Proofreading TIP

Tips for writing a great review

☺	☹
– Describe the place and the activity.	– Insults.
– Say what you liked best and least.	– Include email addresses or phone numbers.
– Tell the readers what to bring (camera, walking shoes...).	– Write in ALL CAPS.
– Say if it's a short visit or an all-day event.	– Report someone else's experience.

Adapted from TripAdvisor.com

Final version

6. Complete the form on the website.

Please provide an overall rating for this attraction: ☆ ☆ ☆ ☆ ☆

Date of your visit: ________ **Were you alone?** ☐ Yes ☐ No

Title your review – If you could say it in one sentence, what would you say?

" ________ "

Your review

____

Does the place have a website?

____

Share

7. Go to TripAdvisor.com, click on "write a review" and send the website your review. Include a photograph of the place, if you have one.

Go to *Looking Back* on page 72 ▶

UNIT 2

Let's go viral!

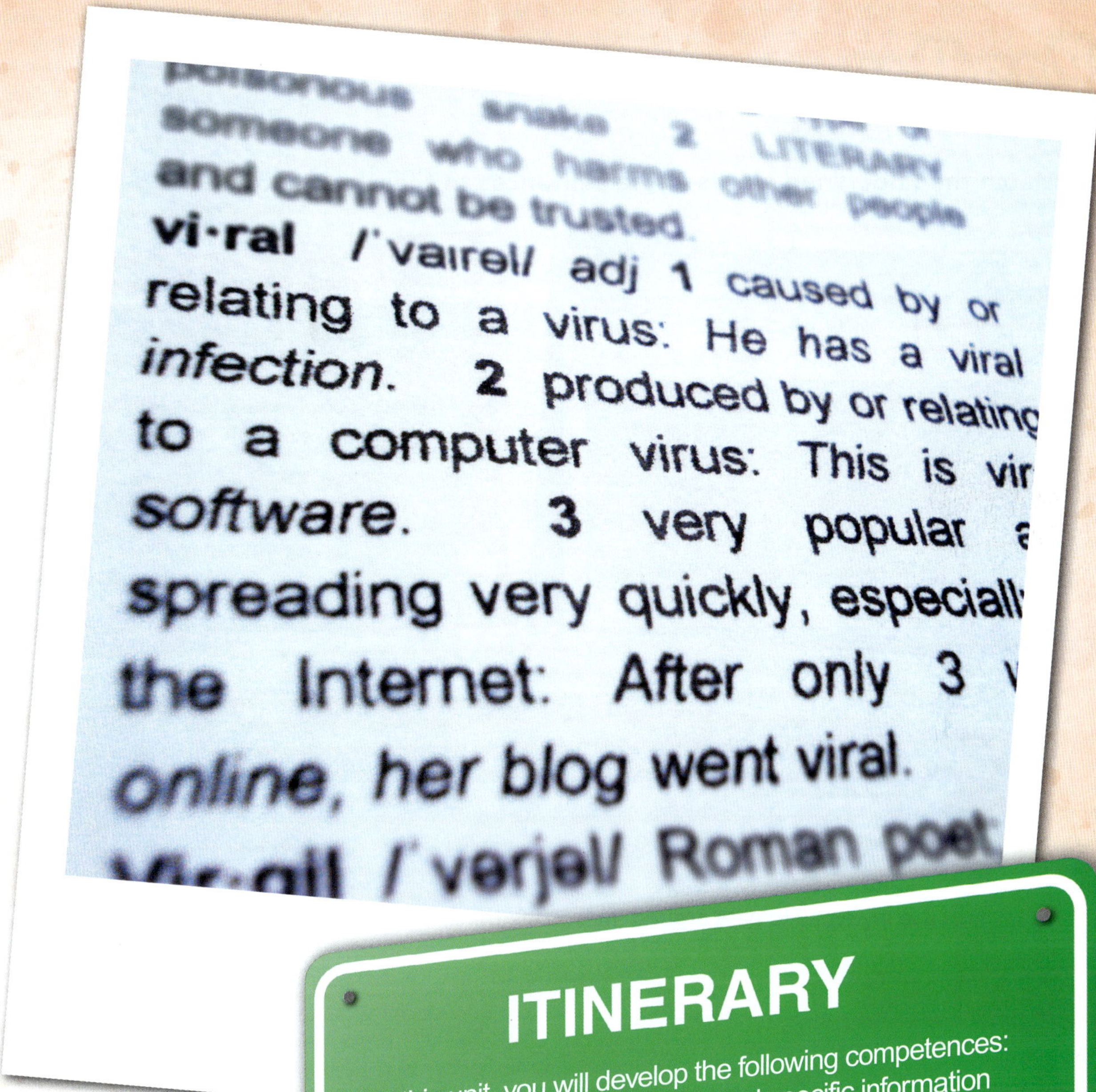

ITINERARY

In this unit, you will develop the following competences:

- reading a FAQ to get general and specific information about memes;
- using the Simple Past to talk about memes and recent fads;
- practicing relaxed pronunciation in informal conversations;
- using *me too / me neither* to agree with a friend's opinion;
- learning words and expressions to describe fads and trends;
- reading a text to understand the relation between genes and memes;
- reflecting on the influence of memes in your learning to identify what is more important and relevant to you;
- listening to a conversation to get general and specific information about the childhood of a group of friends;
- writing a "wanted" poster to make fun of a bad fad.

Reading FAQ

1 Match the underlined words in the sentences to their meanings.

a

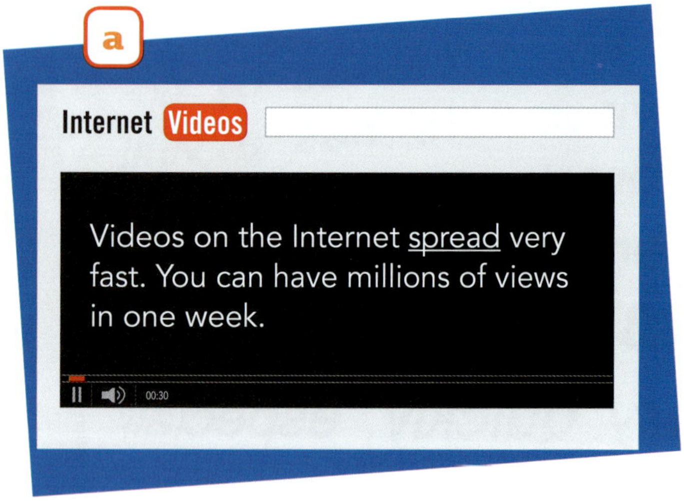

b

c

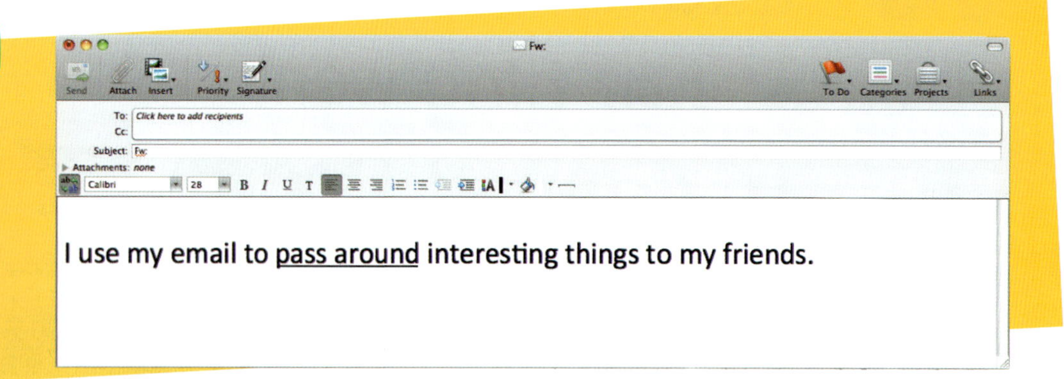

◯ circulate, distribute.

◯ become popular.

◯ disseminate, propagate.

2 What do you know about FAQs? Complete the spaces with one word. The first letter is already there. GENRE

FAQ means "frequently asked q...". It consists of a list of questions and answers about a specific t.. FAQs first appeared on the I.. and the questions and answers were created collaboratively by users. People read them to find the i... they need in a very easy and simple format.

3 **Read the FAQ about memes and match the questions on the next page to the appropriate answer.**

FAQ

✓ ....

A meme is a contagious idea that replicates by parasitically infecting human minds and altering their behavior, causing them to propagate the idea.

✓ ....

The word meme was first used by British evolutionary biologist Richard Dawkins in the book *The Selfish Gene* (1976) to discuss the spread of ideas and cultural phenomena as part of human evolution. The correct pronunciation is /mim/.

✓ ....

Memes are everywhere: on TV, in books, in people's conversations, in songs, on people's clothes, and nowadays the most popular memes are on the Internet.

✓ ....

No, a meme can appear in the form of a behavior, a hyperlink, a video, a picture, a website, a hashtag, or just a word or phrase. And it's not always funny. Funny memes are certainly the most popular ones, but memes can also be dramatic or can be intended to shock.

✓ ....

The first internet meme was a 3-D baby who danced the cha-cha. It appeared in 1996.

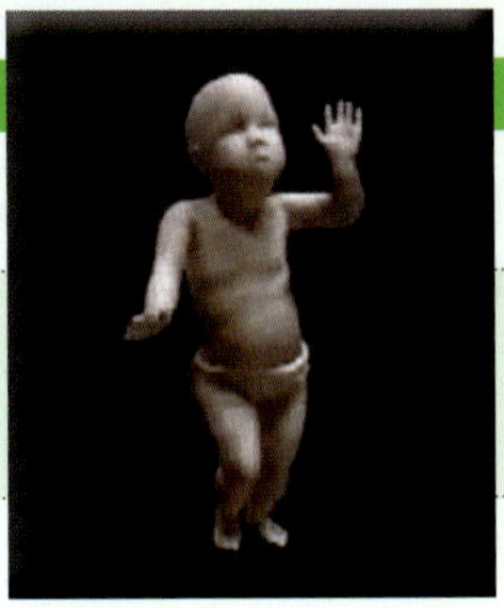

✓ ....

Most memes become infectious accidentally; that is, we usually don't know exactly why some memes catch on and others don't.

✓ ....

Internationally known memes are Lolcats (funny cat pictures with even funnier captions), Rickrolling (a video clip from 80s singer Rick Astley is used as a prank), #fail (when something goes very wrong), Demotivational Posters (original layout of motivational posters, but with funny or absurd texts). In Brazil, some memes that became famous were: #tenso, Dança do Quadrado, Cala a boca Galvão, As árvores somos nozes, #prontofalei, menos Luiza, que está no Canadá etc.

✓ ....

Yes, anyone can try to create a meme. But for your meme to become viral, you need to create something that people want to pass around. Start by studying memes that already exist and then move on to creating one.

Adapted from Memecentral.com, Truthy.Indiana.edu/faq, Memetics.TimTyler.org/faq/

a What are examples of famous internet memes?
b What's the origin of the word "meme" and how is it pronounced?
c What is a meme?
d Is a meme always a funny text?
e Is the transmission of a meme always accidental?
f What was the first internet meme?
g Can I create a meme?
h Where do we find memes?

4 Is it possible for someone to spend his / her life and never be "infected" by a meme? INFER

....

....

....

Grammar Simple Past (II)

1 Read the dialog paying attention to the parts in bold.

Bradley: Hey, Colin. **Did you receive** my email about the Bongo Locos?

Colin: Yes, **I did**. It is really funny! But **I didn't like** the song. Did you like it?

Bradley: No, **I didn't**. But everybody at school is singing the song.

Colin: Really? **I didn't know** that.

2 Answer the questions.

a In Yes / No questions, the correct sequence is...

◯ **did** + verb + subject. ◯ **did** + subject + verb.

b In short answers, we use...

◯ subject + **did** or **didn't**. ◯ subject + **did** or **didn't** + verb.

c In negative sentences, we use...

◯ subject + **didn't** + verb in the past. ◯ subject + **didn't** + verb in the infinitive.

3 Complete the dialog appropriately using the verbs in parentheses.

Marcus: Excuse me. I'm writing an article about internet videos for the school newspaper. Can I ask you some questions?

Silvia: Sure.

Marcus: .... any videos on the Internet because your friends recommended them? (watch)

Silvia: Yes, ...

Marcus: .... them? (like)

Silvia: No, ... I thought they were very stupid.

Marcus: .... the videos to another friend? (send)

Silvia: Yes, ... I sent them by email to Travis here!

Travis: But I .... them because she .... anything in the email, so I imagined it was spam or a virus. (open – write)

Marcus: OK. Thank you guys.

4 **Survey. Make a list of some recent fads in videos, fashion, TV shows, books, etc. Interview three classmates and check if they know about these fads.**

A: Did you listen to Mallu Magalhães's CD?
B: No, I didn't.

A: Did you buy a memory stick?
B: Yes, I did.

Fads	Student 1	Student 2	Student 3

Pronunciation Relaxed pronunciation

Sometimes the words in a sentence are not pronounced clearly or completely and the sounds are mixed together or eliminated, especially in day-to-day informal conversations. We call it relaxed pronunciation.

> **Did you** like it?
> /dɪdʒə /
> (did you sounds like 'didja')

1 **Listen and repeat.** 8

1. **Did you** see it?
2. **Did he** go to the park?
3. **Did they** know the answer?
4. **What did you** do?

Speaking Agreeing

1 **Read and listen to the dialog. Then match the prompts to their equivalent meanings.** 9

Mike: I hated this movie.
Brian: **Me too**. I didn't understand the story.
Mike: **Me neither**. And I didn't like the actors.

a Me too. ◯ I didn't understand the story.
b Me neither. ◯ I hated the movie.

Agreeing with affirmative sentences	Agreeing with negative sentences
Me too.	Me neither.

To disagree, use short answers. See page 29.

A: I **liked** the movie.
B: I **didn't**.

A: I **didn't** like the movie.
B: I **did**.

2 Listen and repeat the conversations. 10

A: I watched the movie Rango.

B: Me too. | B: I didn't.

A: I didn't watch the movie Rango.

B: Me neither. | B: I did.

3 Practice the dialog in pairs.

a Student A: Make true sentences about yourself using the prompts below. Does Student B agree or disagree with you?

Student B: Go to page 148.

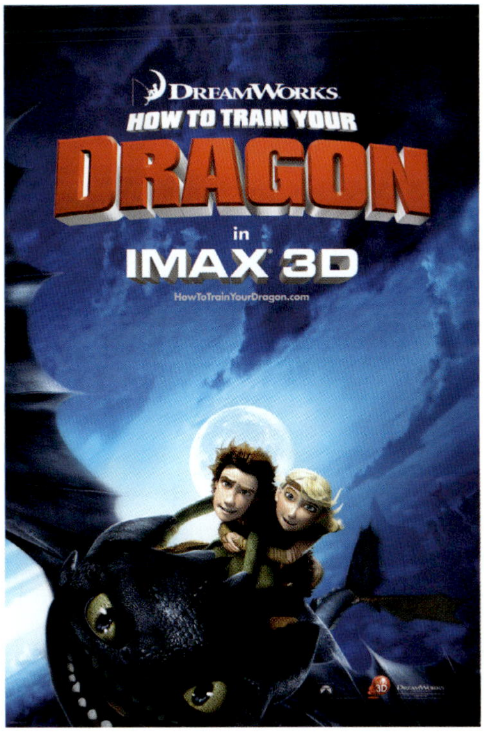

1 I ***watched / didn't watch*** the movie *How To Train Your Dragon.*

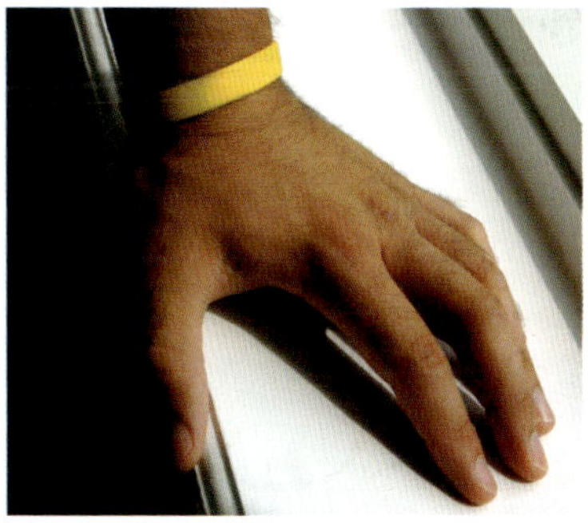

2 I ***bought / didn't buy*** the yellow wristbands.

3 I ***played / didn't play*** social games where you manage a farm.

b Student A: Listen to Student B. Agree or disagree with him / her using short sentences.

Vocabulary

Fads and trends in the 2000s – Brazil

1 Write the words next to the correct picture. Then listen to check your answers. 11

watch stand up comedy • play Sudoku • have bangs • do cosplay • wear retro sunglasses • have a mohawk • use an SD card • have roller shoes • wear skinny pants

a ....

b ....

c ....

d ....

e ....

f ....

g ....

h ....

i ....

2 Write true sentences about you (or the people you know) and the fads.

I didn't have a mohawk.

My brother played sudoku.

....

....

....

....

166

Science | Crossroads | English

1 Answer the questions.

a Do you know what a gene is?

....

b What do you think genes and memes have in common?

....

....

2 Read the text about genes and do the activities.

What are genes?

The human body is made of cells that have different sizes and functions. Inside every cell we have the genes which we received from our parents. Genes give instructions to the cells of what and how they have to do something; for example "be a red blood cell".

Genes are the smallest part of a molecule called DNA (Deoxyribo nucleic acid). The DNA is organized in pieces called chromosomes. When people say, "You have your mother's eyes!", they are actually saying: "You probably inherited a gene (or genes) from your mother that makes a protein that gives the instruction to your eyes to have the same color as your mother's eyes." But 95.5% of the DNA of every person on the planet is the same. We have more in common than you imagined!

Adapted from Neok12.com

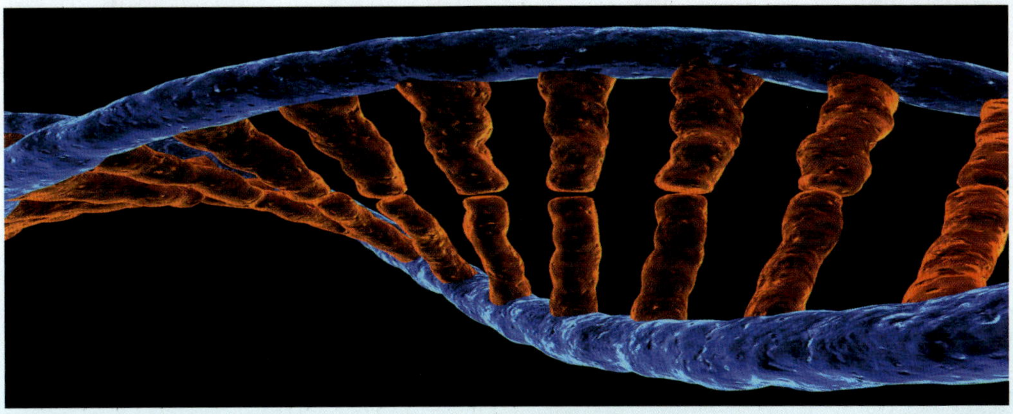

DNA

a Order the 3 items in order of size (**1** is the smallest, **3** is the biggest).

◯ DNA ◯ gene ◯ chromosome

b Rewrite the sentence in a more informal way.

"You probably inherited a gene (or genes) from your father that makes a protein that gives the instruction to your hair to be the same as your father's."

....

BY THE WAY...

There isn't a relationship between the number of chromosomes and the number of genes. So, believe it or not, goldfish (94) and toucans (106) have more chromosomes than people (46)!

Adapted from Home.EarthLink.net

166

↑ Road to success

Memes in education

Podemos aplicar o conceito de meme ao aprendizado.

Muitas das ideias que temos sobre a melhor maneira de aprender um idioma nos foram passadas por nossos pais, professores, colegas de classe e até mesmo pela sociedade. Alguns memes, como "Você só vai aprender inglês se estudar nos Estados Unidos" ou "Um professor nativo é melhor" não vão ajudar muito. Por isso, procure identificar quais memes são mais eficientes ou mais relevantes para você.

Listening When I was a child...

1 **Listen to these friends talking about the past. Check the image that illustrates the main topic of the conversation.** 12 SKIM

a ◯

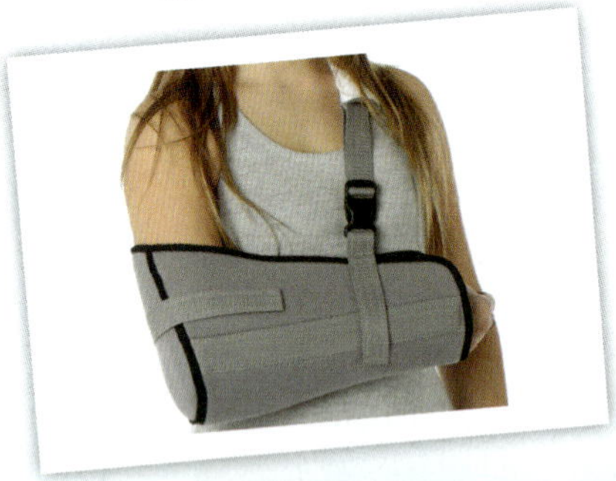

b ◯

c ◯

2 Listen again and answer. (12) SCAN

a Did all the girls have scooters?

....

b What color was Jenna's scooter?

....

c Molly didn't have a bike. Why?

....

d How many times did Emily break her arm?

....

Writing Wanted poster for a bad fad

One of the oldest written viral messages ever created was Wanted posters. Originally, the objective of Wanted posters was to let the public know of a criminal that authorities were looking for. But the posters – especially the ones in old-west style – became so popular that people started using them in many humorous ways as a creative way to analyze something or someone.

Preparing to write

1. Choose a bad fad that you never liked.
2. Think about the reason this fad is bad.

Draft

3. Make a draft of your poster. Be creative! Remember it's a humorous poster, so people who read it need to find it funny!
4. Proofread your text.

Final version

5. Make the final version of your poster on a piece of cardboard or use an online generator: GlassGiant.com

Share

6. Make your poster go viral. Share it with as many friends as possible!

Go to *Looking Back* on page 72 ▶

Stopover Units 1 & 2

1 **Complete the grid with appropriate words and find out the name of the largest mall in the world.**

hang out with										
have										
go to the										
sing										
surf the										
stay										
hang out at the										
swim at the										
go										

The .... is located in the United Arab Emirates and has a total area of 350,000 m².

2 **Connect the letters and find six verbs in the past. You can't jump a square.**

B	U	G	H	T
G	O	N	C	K
T	A	V	E	N
D	L	W	D	O
E	K	K	O	T

3 Crosswords.

Extra Reading 1

"Don't Stop Believin'", a song from 1981 by Journey, gained meme status after it was used in many TV shows and movies such as *Glee, The Sopranos, Family Guy, Scrubs, South Park, King of the Hill, Cold Case, CSI: Crime Scene Investigation, My Name Is Earl, Just Shoot Me, Laguna Beach, The Wedding Singer* (1998), *Shrek the Halls* (2007), and *Bedtime Stories* (2008).

It was the first song from the pre-digital era to sell more than 2 million downloads through a famous online digital media store.

1 Read the lyrics and answer: What is this song about?

Don't Stop Believin'

by Journey

Just a small town girl
living' in a lonely world
She took the midnight train goin'
anywhere
Just a city boy, born and raised in
South Detroit
He took the midnight train goin'
anywhere

A singer in a smoky room
The smell of wine and cheap perfume
For a smile they can share the night
It goes on and on and on and on

Strangers waiting
Up and down the boulevard
Their shadows searching in the night
Streetlights, people
Living just to find emotion
Hiding somewhere in the night

Working hard to get my fill
Everybody wants a thrill
Paying anything to roll the dice
Just one more time

Some will win, some will lose
Some are born to sing the blues
And now the movie never ends
It goes on and on and on and on

Don't stop believin'
Hold on to that feelin'
Streetlight, people
(repeat)

a ◯ Two people traveling to another city.
b ◯ Two people who are looking for a better life.
c ◯ Two people who are working hard.

2 Match these expressions to their meanings.

a Born and raised
b Get my fill
c To sing the blues
d Hold on to something

◯ To be satisfied, to have enough of something.
◯ Maintain something, preserve something.
◯ To be born and nurtured through childhood, usually in a specific place.
◯ To be sad and melancholic.

3 What words below do you relate to the lyrics of the song? Justify.

◯ optimistic
◯ pessimistic
◯ depressing
◯ emotional
◯ evasive

4 In an article about the song "Don't Stop Believin'", journalist Dorian Lynskey describes it this way:

"So first it was a normal song, then a forgotten one, then an ironic reference, then a genuine comeback, then a phenomenon, and now it's just there, like the sun or gravity or 'Hey Jude'."

From Guardian.co.uk

---

a What does he imply about the public opinion of the song?

....

....

b What does he mean when he compares "Don't Stop Believin'" with "Hey Jude"?

....

....

....

Project 1

Time capsules

A time capsule is a historic archive of objects and information.

The objective of a time capsule is to communicate with the future: people from the present can help future archaeologists, anthropologists, and historians understand the past. After people create a time capsule, they close it, hide it, and set a date for it to be reopened.

There are many closed time capsules in the world, waiting for their opening date. One of the most famous ones is called Crypt of Civilization and it's in Atlanta, USA. The Crypt of Civilization was closed in 1940 and it can only be reopened on May 28th, 8113!

1 **Look at the interior of the Crypt of Civilization and answer the questions.**

a What do you think people included in this time capsule?

b How do you think people in 8113 will react when they see the contents of 1940?

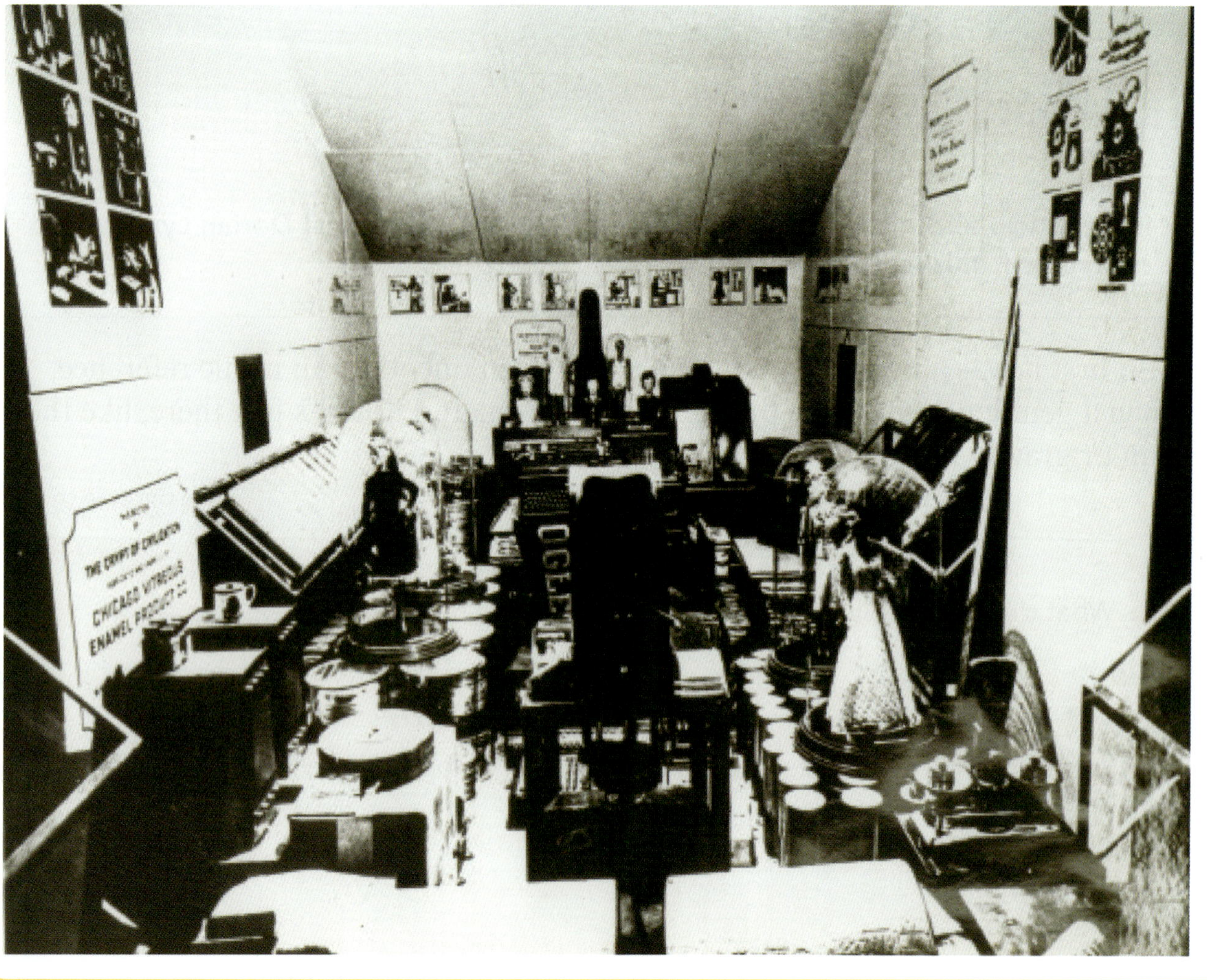

2 Create your own time capsule!

a First, use the categories below to make a list of objects and information you want to include in your time capsule. **Remember:** All the objects and information you choose need to be relevant **now**.

Photos	
Videos	
Newspapers / magazines	
Objects	
Fads / memes	
Recordings	

b Think about the reasons why you chose these items.
c Choose a name for your time capsule.
d Pick a date for the reopening of your time capsule.
e Collect all the material you listed.
f Present the content of your time capsule to your classmates. Be prepared to explain why you chose those items.
g Put all the items in a box and seal it.

If you don't want to leave certain objects in the time capsule, leave a photograph of the object. Write the name of your time capsule on the box and the date for the reopening. Leave your time capsule in a safe place.

UNIT 3
Be kind to one another

ITINERARY

In this unit, you will develop the following competences:

- reading campaign posters to get general and specific information and infer about discrimination;
- learning words and expressions to talk about prejudice;
- developing acceptance and understanding of other cultures to communicate better;
- practicing the sounds of the letter "x" to pronounce some words appropriately;
- reading about the Universal Declaration of Human Rights to reflect about the situation in your country;
- using expressions to respond to senseless and irrational arguments;
- listening to a police dispatch call to get general and specific information about crime;
- using *must, might, should,* and *might want to* to talk about tolerance and respect;
- writing a campaign poster to protest.

Reading

Noncommercial campaign posters

1 **A campaign is a series of advertisement messages that share the same idea and marketing strategy. What do you know about noncommercial campaign posters? Check what is true about them.** GENRE

- **a** ◯ Noncommercial campaign posters can be published by organizations like NGOs (nongovernmental organizations), for example.
- **b** ◯ They don't have a slogan.
- **c** ◯ Campaign posters are not political.
- **d** ◯ They use a variety of media channels (posters, magazines, newspapers, billboards, etc).
- **e** ◯ They frequently use very meaningful images.
- **f** ◯ The objective is to get the attention of readers and encourage them to learn more about the topic of the ad.

2 **Circle the option to make the sentences true in your opinion.**

a Most TV commercials about cleaning products show a **woman** / **man** using the product.

b Most dolls sold in Brazil are **white** / **black**.

c The color pink is associated with **heterosexuals** / **homosexuals** / **everyone**.

d **It is** / **It is not** important to dress nicely after you turn 40.

3 **Share your answers on activity 2 with a classmate. Do your answers reflect a discriminatory attitude? Explain.**

....

....

4 **Read the introduction and the ads. Can you identify the type of discrimination in each ad?** SCAN

First Ad: ....

Second Ad: ....

Third Ad: ....

An anti-discrimination agency initiated a massive poster campaign across the city of Amsterdam, Netherlands, to initiate a dialog about and protest against discrimination.

Advertising Agency: imagine', Amsterdam, Netherlands
Art Director: Sander Jacobs
Copywriter: Sander Bergmeijer
Director: Mike van Diem
Photographer: Oscar Seijkens

5 **Can you guess the meaning of the word "hide", based on the idea of these ads?**

....

....

BY THE WAY...

"Should you have to hide the real you to be accepted?" is a rhetorical question. A **rhetorical question** is not a real question because it doesn't need an answer. Its objective is to encourage the reader (or the listener) to think about the obvious answer. An effective rhetorical question can persuade the reader (or the listener) to believe in the position of the writer (or the speaker).

6 **Do these ads use rhetorical questions effectively? Why (not)?** INFER

....

....

YOUR TAKE

Do you think these types of discrimination are a problem only in the Netherlands?

....

"Discrimination is not only harmful for individuals but for society as a whole." Do you agree or disagree with that? Why?

....

Vocabulary Prejudice

1 **Match these words to their meanings. Then listen to check your answers.** 13

a sexism	( ) discrimination based on a person's age
b racism	( ) the belief that one gender (male or female) is inferior, less competent, or less valuable
c ageism	( ) intense aversion to people from other countries
d homophobia	( ) intense aversion to people from other religions
e xenophobia	( ) extreme aversion to homosexuality
f religious intolerance	( ) the belief that one race is superior to others

Attention!

sexism (noun)	–	sexist (adjective)
racism (noun)	–	racist (adjective)
ageism (noun)	–	ageist (adjective)
homophobia (noun)	–	homophobic (adjective)
xenophobia (noun)	–	xenophobic (adjective)
religious intolerance (noun)	–	intolerant (adjective)

2 **Write what each sign is protesting against.**

EVERYONE
is a foreigner
SOMEWHERE!

....

equality

....

If you don't like
gay marriage,
BLAME **straight** people.
They are the ones who keep having gay babies.

....

....

....

....

166

↑ Road to success

Language and culture

Um idioma representa ideias, culturas e ideologias de uma sociedade. Por isso, quando aprendemos uma língua nova, temos que aprender também a entender a cultura dos países falantes, em geral muito diferente da nossa.

Antes de julgar ou criticar uma cultura diferente, lembre-se de que a diversidade de culturas nos enriquece e nos torna pessoas melhores. Cultivar a compreensão, a aceitação e o respeito às diferentes culturas nos permite uma comunicação melhor e evita conflitos, confrontos e até mesmo guerras!

Pronunciation The sound of the letter *x*

1 In English, the letter *x* has four possible pronunciations. Listen to the examples. (14)

TAXI – sound of ks, /ks/

LUXURY – sound of ksh, /kʃ/

XENOPHOBIA – sound of z, /z/

EXAMPLE – sound of gz, /gz/

2 Listen and repeat each group of words and match them with their sound of *x*. (15)

a	anxiety – xerox – xylophone	◯	/ks/
b	sexual – complexion – anxious	◯	/z/
c	exhibition – oxygen – ex	◯	/kʃ/
d	exaggerate – exact – executive	◯	/gz/

BY THE WAY...

The letter **x** has many other uses:

- In mathematics, it expresses an unknown value: 10 + x = 34.
- In Roman numbers, it represents the number 10: MMX = 2010.
- It's the name of a chromosome that decides the human gender: women have two X-chromosomes; men have one X-chromosome.
- In informal writing, it means "a kiss": XOXO = kiss, hug, kiss, hug.
- It comes before a hyphen in some English words: X-ray, X-rated.
- It's an abbreviation for **cheese** in Portuguese: *x-burguer*, *x-salada*.

History | Crossroads | English

1 **What do you understand by "human rights"?**

....

....

....

....

2 **In your opinion, which rights are protected by the Declaration?**

- ◯ The right to not be discriminated because of your religion.
- ◯ The right to not be discriminated because of your race.
- ◯ The right to not be discriminated because of your sexuality.
- ◯ The right to not be discriminated because of your gender.
- ◯ The right to not be discriminated because of your social status.

3 **Read some articles of The Universal Declaration of Human Rights and match them to their summaries.**

We have the right to believe in what we want to believe. ....

We have the right to marry and have a family if we want. ....

We are all born free and equal. ....

We have freedom of expression. ....

We're all equal before the law. ....

We can't discriminate. ....

The Universal Declaration of Human Rights

In 1945, after the extermination of millions of people because of their race, religion, physical conditions, and sexual orientation during World War II, governments established an international organization which should prevent these things from happening again: the United Nations (U.N.).

In 1948 the U.N. created The Universal Declaration of Human Rights to protect people's rights to life, freedom, basic necessities, and nationality.

Article 1

- All human beings are born free and equal in dignity and rights. They are endowed with reason and conscience and should act towards one another in a spirit of brotherhood.

Article 2

- Everyone is entitled to all the rights and freedoms set forth in this Declaration, without distinction of any kind, such as race, color, sex, language, religion, political, or other opinion, national or social origin, property, birth, or other status. Furthermore, no distinction shall be made on the basis of the political, jurisdictional, or international status of the country or territory to which a person belongs, whether it be independent, trust, non-self-governing, or under any other limitation of sovereignty.

(...)

Article 7

- All are equal before the law and are entitled without any discrimination to equal protection of the law. All are entitled to equal protection against any discrimination in violation of this Declaration and against any incitement to such discrimination.

(...)

Article 16

- (1) Men and women of full age, without any limitation due to race, nationality, or religion, have the right to marry and to found a family. They are entitled to equal rights as to marriage, during marriage, and at its dissolution.

(...)

Article 18

- Everyone has the right to freedom of thought, conscience, and religion; this right includes freedom to change his religion or belief, and freedom, either alone, or in community with others and in public or private, to manifest his religion or belief in teaching, practice, worship, and observance.

Article 19

- Everyone has the right to freedom of opinion and expression; this right includes freedom to hold opinions without interference and to seek, receive, and impart information and ideas through any media and regardless of frontiers.

From UN.org

YOUR TAKE

1. Look for information or photos in newspapers or magazines where a human right is being demanded, respected, or denied. Cut the examples out and stick them on a piece of cardboard.
2. Think about what right is involved in each situation. Read a copy of The Universal Declaration of Human Rights and find an article that matches the situation. Write the text of this article next to the images on the cardboard.
3. Share your posters with your classmates.

Speaking Responding to senseless / irrational arguments

1 Listen and read. 17

Teacher: Your composition is not good. You should learn how to write with the girls in this class.
Student: That's very sexist, Mr. Tyler. You might want to reconsider that.

More informal	More polite
That's so wrong! That's absurd! You must be out of your mind!	I can't agree with that. You should think it over. You might want to reconsider that. You might regret these words in the future.

2 In pairs, respond to these senseless / irrational arguments. Choose a more appropriate answer according to the people involved.

1. Washing the dishes is a girl's job; boys should never do it!
2. The Japanese and Chinese are superior because they are more intelligent than others.
3. Our grandparents are just too old to understand technology.
4. Immigrants shouldn't have the same job opportunities as locals.
5. My religion is the best one and it's the only one that is correct.
6. Lesbians are nothing but women who couldn't get a husband.
7. Men can't love, they are all insensitive.

a mother and son

Son: Washing the dishes is a girl's job; boys should never do it!
Mother: What? Don't be sexist! That's absurd!

b father and son / daughter
c two best friends
d two neighbors who are not close
e principal and student
f two classmates

3 Are there any manifestations of prejudice in your community? In groups, discuss what you can do to promote respect. Then share your ideas with the class.

Listening Police dispatchers

1 **Police dispatchers (or 911 operators) answer emergency calls, contact, and send police officers, police cars, or ambulances to the appropriate locations. Listen to this call and answer: what was the reason for this attack?** 16 SKIM

a ◯ Religious intolerance.
b ◯ Racial intolerance.
c ◯ Social intolerance.
d ◯ Sexual intolerance.

2 **Listen again and answer.** 16 SCAN

a the emergency service requested:
◯ ambulance ◯ police officers ◯ firefighters

b number of victims: ....

c age of victim(s): ....

d gender of victim(s): ◯ male ◯ female

e causes: ◯ car accident ◯ robbery ◯ physically attacked

f number of suspects that attacked the victim: ....

YOUR TAKE

What are the emergency telephone numbers in your city?

....

Grammar *Must / might / should*

1 **Read the sentences. Then underline the correct answers.**

You **must** be tolerant and respectful of all religions.
You **should** think it over.
You **might want to** reconsider that.
You **might** regret these words in the future.

Negative forms

- *must not / mustn't*
- *might not*
- *should not / shouldn't*

a *Must* expresses ***possibility / advice / obligation***.
b *Might* expresses ***possibility / advice / obligation***.
c *Might want to* expresses ***possibility / advice / obligation***.
d *Should* expresses ***possibility / advice / obligation***.

2 Complete the dialogs with *should*, *must*, or *might want to*.

Paul: Hi Ana! What are you doing?

Ana: I'm trying to write a composition about human rights for my English class. But it's very difficult!

Paul: The Universal Declaration of Human Rights says that we .... respect all people, regardless of their race, age, religion, etc. right?

Ana: Yes, I know that, but that's all I know!

Paul: You .... research first. You .... find useful information to use in your composition.

Ana: That's true! Thanks!

Charlie: Cesar is very late. I think we .... go without him.

Paula: He .... be lost; he's very bad with directions, just like all men.

Charlie: Oh, please, that's absurd and sexist!

Man: We .... (not) judge someone because of his or her nationality.

Girl: Why not?

Man: Because a person's character is not defined by the place where he or she is born.

Girl: Why not?

Man: Because a person's character .... be a result of their education, not their nationality.

Girl: Why?

Man: OK, Amanda, stop with the questions now. It's late; we .... go home!

Writing A campaign poster

Preparing to write

1. Read the characteristics of a campaign poster on page 44 again.
2. Choose one (or more than one) prejudice that you want to protest against. (you might use ideas on page 46).
3. Who's the target audience of your poster? (Are you writing for teens, adults, children, everyone?)
4. Where are you going to display your poster?

Draft

5. Write your poster.
6. Proofread your text.

Proofreading TIP

Writing slogans can be hard. So, here are some tips to help you revise your campaign slogan.

- **Does it have rhythm and rhyme?**
  Slogans should be good to hear. Rhythmic slogans are much more recognizable and memorable. Bonus points if you can make the slogan into a jingle or song: words presented in a song are remembered better than words presented in normal speech.
  Corruption leads to our destruction. → campaign against corruption
  You use, you lose. → campaign against drug abuse

- **Is it short?**
  Slogans should never be longer than a sentence and ideally should work between six to eight words. Short sentences are easier to remember, which is the objective of slogan writing.
  Extinct is forever. → campaign for saving endangered species
  Save water! Save life! → campaign for saving water supplies

- **Can you make it funny?**
  If you can't make it funny without making it ridiculous, just forget the funny and go with the other options.
  Eat beans not beings. → campaign for vegetarianism
  Cancer cures smoking. → campaign against smoking

- **Did you play with words?**
  If you didn't and you want to try it, write down on small pieces of paper words related to the topic. Play around with them: organize them in different ways and make a list of the good ideas you see. Word play is the best way to write an original slogan.
  Cool kids help a warm planet. → campaign for stopping global warming
  Fast! Food for All. → campaign against hunger

Final version

7. Write the final version of your poster. Include images and make sure you include where to find more information on the topic (a web address, for example).

Share

8. Display your poster. If you want to display your poster somewhere outside the school (like in a store or in the mall), make sure you have authorization to do that.

Go to *Looking Back* on page 73 ▶

UNIT 4

You are what you eat

ITINERARY

In this unit, you will develop the following competences:

- reading an article to learn about how cookies are made;
- learning words and collocations to describe food;
- listening to a dialog to get general and specific information about the Girl Scouts cookies;
- using expressions and emphasis to agree and disagree;
- using the passive voice to talk about food;
- reading an article to learn more about how food can affect your school performance;
- developing the habit of drinking water to help you in your school performance;
- writing a menu plan to help you follow a healthy diet.

Reading How cookies are made

1 Look at the pictures and answer the questions.

1

2

3

4

5

6

7

a Which one is your favorite? ....

b What do you call them in your city? ....

c Do you or your family make cookies at home? ....

d Which of these ingredients do you think are included in a sandwich cookie recipe (picture I)?

◯ flour

◯ cocoa powder

◯ oatmeal

◯ baking soda

e Read the text on the next page and check your answers in letter **d**.

2 Read the text again and answer the questions. SCAN

a Where was the sandwich cookie created?

....

b What are the ingredients of sandwich cookies?

....

3 In the text, find and circle the key words below. Then match each word with its meaning.

filling • batter • dough • wrap • cool down

a A liquid mixture of flour, milk (or water), eggs, etc. ....

b A thick mixture of flour, milk (or water), eggs, etc. ....

c A food mixture that goes into something. ....

d To cover and protect. ....

e To become cold or less hot. ....

How are sandwich cookies made?

In 1908, an American biscuit company had the idea of putting two chocolate wafers together, with a sweet filling in between. The *sandwich cookie* was born.

Billions of cookies are produced every year in the United States, which is the main cookie market of the world. Brazil holds the second position, in absolute terms, with a six-kilogram-a-year consumption per person.

Granulated sugar, cocoa powder, salt, oil, water, and leavening ingredients (like baking soda) are mixed together to form the batter.

Dry ice is added to cool down the mixture to room temperature. That will guarantee the cookies are crumbly. Flour is incorporated into the batter to form the dough.

The dough is pressed into a molding machine that not only cuts the wafers in the right shape, but also prints designs on them.

The wafers are baked in a gas oven for some minutes and then cooled down by fans. That makes them crispy.

A special machine deposits the filling on them and joins the two wafers together.

The sandwich cookies are separated into bunches and then released into plastic trays. These trays are wrapped in metallic film, and the packages are hot sealed.

Adapted from Discovery Channel's show "How it's made"; BrazzilMag.com/news

YOUR TAKE

Did you know that Brazil holds the second position in the cookie market? Why do you think cookies are so popular in Brazil?

Vocabulary Food collocations

1 **Read these words to describe food. Then complete the sentences.**

sweet

granulated

crumbly

crispy

dry

a These words are…

◯ verbs.
◯ adjectives.
◯ nouns.

b They are used to…

◯ order food. ◯ describe food. ◯ talk about food quantity.

> **Attention!**
> People say "a crispy chip", but they normally don't say "a crumbly chip". The limited possibilities of word combination is called **collocation**.

2 **Study the food descriptions below.**

Gelatin is **soft** and **sweet**.

Crackers are **salty**, **dry**, and **crumbly**.

Chips are **crispy**.

3 **Match the foods below with adjectives that can describe them then listen and check your work. Some foods have more than one possible adjective.** 18

sugar • cookies • fried chicken • chips • milk shake • candy • chocolate • crackers • ricotta cheese • gelatin

Taste		Texture				
sweet	salty	granulated	crispy	dry	soft	crumbly
....	....	....	....	....	....	....
....	....	....	....	....	....	....
....	....	....	....	....	....	....
....	....	....	....	....	....	....
....	....	....	....	....	....	....

Listening Girl Scouts

1 Look at the picture of a Girl Scout. Do you know what activities Girl Scouts do? Read the paragraph below and check.

The Girl Scouts of the United States of America (GSUSA) is a youth organization for girls in the United States. It describes itself as "the world's preeminent organization dedicated solely to girls". The Girl Scouts cookies are sold to raise funds. Once a year, the Girl Scouts volunteer to sell cookies from door to door. The money they receive is used to fund activities such as community service, summer camps, projects, trips, and events for the community.

2 Listen to a conversation between a Girl Scout and a potential buyer. Does she sell the cookies? 19 SKIM

....

3 Listen again and answer the questions. 19 SCAN

a How many boxes did he buy?

....

b How much did he spend?

....

c What arguments convinced him to buy the cookies?

....

YOUR TAKE

Do you agree that cookies make a good gift? On which occasions could you give them as gifts?

....

Would you buy cookies or any other food to help a cause?

....

BY THE WAY...

One of the main goals of the Girl Scouts Cookie Program is to teach the girls about money management.
The Girl Scouts take cookie orders, handle customers' money, and gain valuable and practical lessons around financial literacy. They also have to be careful with how they spend the money they receive because it has to last a whole year.
And you? How can you learn about money management?

Speaking & Pronunciation

Agreeing and disagreeing / Emphasis

1 **Two friends are talking about their options for dinner. Listen to the dialog. Then underline the sentences used to agree and circle the ones used to disagree.** 20

Jenny: You want to eat sandwiches for dinner? No way! That's not a meal!

Lauren: Yes, it is! It depends on the type of sandwich you make.

Jenny: I'm not so sure about that. I mean, I love sandwiches, but don't you think that there are better options?

Lauren: Absolutely! But that's not the point! People don't consider a sandwich a meal because of the choices they make. But there are natural ingredients that can make a sandwich a healthy option.

Jenny: Not necessarily. Depending on the combination, you can have lots of fat or lots of calories. Just because something is natural, it doesn't mean it is healthy.

Lauren: I guess so. People use the word "natural" in the wrong way, I guess. But that doesn't change the fact that some sandwiches can be better than unhealthy meals.

Jenny: That's so true. Hey… Why don't you prepare some of your healthy sandwiches so that I can change my opinion about them?

Lauren: That's exactly what I was thinking! There's some avocado and shrimp… hmm… let me think…

2 **Listen and pay attention to the stressed words.** 21

a No <u>way</u>!

b I'm <u>not</u> so sure about that.

3 **Listen and underline the stressed words.** 22

a Absolutely! But that's not the point!

b Not necessarily.

c I guess so.

d That's so true.

e That's exactly what I was thinking!

4 Discuss the topic below. Use the expressions you learned to agree or disagree with your partner.

It is OK to encourage people to consume cookies, considered as junk food, for a good cause.

Student A: Go to page 149.
Student B: Imagine you disagree with the statement above. Use the arguments below and try to convince Student A.

- People will probably eat them if they are available.
- The Girl Scouts should ask for money donations; they shouldn't sell the cookies to raise money.
- People should donate money, not junk food, to help poor children.
- The Girl Scouts should raise money by selling something healthier. Fruit, for example.

YOUR TAKE

Considering all the arguments you know now, how do you respond to the argument on **activity 4**?

....

....

Grammar Passive voice

1 Read the sentences below and do the activities.

I. American companies **produce** billions of cookies every year.
II. Billions of cookies **are produced** every year.
III. Girl Scouts **sold** a box of chocolate cookies for U$ 4 last year.
IV. Last year a box of the chocolate Girl Scout cookies **was sold** for U$ 4.

a Sentences .... and .... are in the present, and sentences .... and .... are in the past.

b Do we know the subject of sentences 1 and 3? Underline them in the sentences. ....

c In sentences 2 and 4, is the subject clear? ....

2 Look at the diagrams of two kinds of sentence and complete the sentences.

Active Voice			
subject	main verb (in the present or past)	object	complement

Passive Voice		
object	Verb to be (in the present or past) + main verb (in the past participle)	complement

a In activity 1, sentences .... are in the active voice and sentences .... are in the passive voice.

b We use the .... voice when we don't know, don't need or don't want to mention who does the action.

3 Read the sentences below. Write AV if they are in the active voice, or PV if they are in the passive voice.

a The Asians started banana cultivation around 5000 BC. ◯

b The kiwi was originally called Chinese gooseberry, and it was renamed in the 1950s. ◯

c The heaviest watermelon in the world weighs around 119 kg. ◯

d Dried jackfruit chips are produced by various manufacturers around the world. ◯

e Filipinos use pineapple fiber to make furniture. ◯

f The pomegranate is cultivated as bonsais in Japan and China. ◯

4 **Complete the text with the verbs in the passive voice in the present or past.**

Typical Brazilian dishes

Vatapá

Vatapá .... (bring) by Africans to Brazil in the 16th century. In Brazil, new ingredients .... (incorporate) to the original recipe. Nowadays, it .... (prepare) with fish, shrimp, or chicken.

Pato no tucupi

It .... (associate) with the *Círio de Nazaré*, a big celebration in Pará.
The dish .... (make) with *tucupi*, a yellow broth that .... (extract) from cassava. After cooking the duck, it .... (cut) into pieces and boiled in *tucupi* for some time. It .... (serve) with white rice and manioc flour.

Quindim

It .... (create) by African slaves in the 17th century when sugar plantations .... (find) everywhere in Brazil and coconut was abundant.
It .... (make) with egg yolks, an influence of Portuguese cuisine.

5 **Research about another typical Brazilian dish and write sentences about it, using the passive voice.**

....

....

....

....

....

....

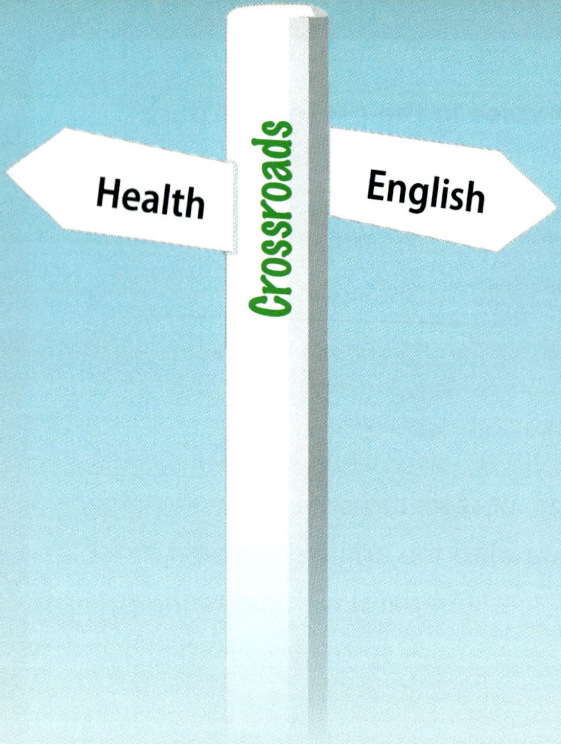

167

Jamie Oliver is a British chef and TV personality famous for his cooking shows and his campaigns against the use of processed foods in schools.

1 What do you know about the way food affects your school performance? Check what you believe is true.

- ◯ Healthy food helps to improve exam results.
- ◯ Healthy food helps to improve classroom attendance.
- ◯ Healthy food doesn't make you calmer.
- ◯ Red meat, beans, and green vegetables improve your cognitive development and concentration.
- ◯ Dishes like pasta and fruit don't give students energy.

2 Read the article and check which sentences from activity 1 are correct.

Jamie's food fuels students' brain power

It seems Jamie Oliver knows best. New research suggests the celebrity chef's healthy school dinners have helped to improve exam results and classroom attendance.

An independent study shows the performance of 11-year-old pupils eating Oliver's meals improved by up to 8% in science and 6% in English, while absenteeism related to ill-health fell by 15%.

This weekend Oliver said: "We could see the benefits to children's health while doing the program: it made them calmer and consequently able to learn. The results are fantastic – it's the first time a proper study was done into the positive effects of the Feed Me Better campaign. It strongly suggests we were right."

During the campaign, Oliver hired nutritionists who found most school meals contained less than half the daily recommended amount of iron, a mineral that improves children's cognitive development and concentration. In response, the chef introduced iron-rich foods such as red meat, beans and green vegetables, while reducing sugar and saturated fat by eliminating processed foods.

Oliver's new menus, adopted by 81 out of 88 primary and secondary schools in Greenwich, included more pasta and fresh fruit, plus dishes such as Mexican bean wraps, chickpea soup, and vegetable chow mein. Hayley Franklin, 11, from John Roan school in Blackheath, southeast London, said: "The new dinners give me much more energy, for longer, so I can concentrate on work through the whole day."

Adapted from TimesOnline.co.uk

3 Do the results of the research surprise you? Explain.

....

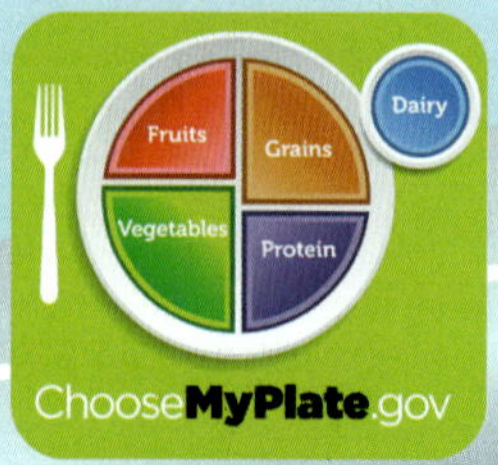

4 Look at the healthy food icon used by the United States government. It shows the amount of each food category that you should eat in every meal. How do you compare your meals with the one from the icon?

↑ Road to success

Think water

Você sabia que, dentre todos os órgãos em nossos corpos, o cérebro é o que contém mais água?

Não é possível substituir a ingestão de água por bebidas como refrigerantes, sucos, café e chá, pois elas são diuréticas e são processadas pelo nosso corpo como se fossem comida. Quando estamos desidratados, nosso cérebro tem mais dificuldade para processar informações e acabamos entediados, desanimados e desconcentrados. Por isso, lembre-se de beber água nos intervalos entre as aulas e, se possível, tenha sempre uma garrafa de água na sala de aula.

Writing A healthy menu plan

When you plan your weekly menu, you have the opportunity to think about what you eat, balance your diet according to your needs and preferences, and avoid the foods that are bad for you. Planning ahead helps you make healthier choices, and it saves money.

Preparing to write

1. Analyze the "Choose Your Plate" icon on page 64 again.
2. Make a list of foods that fit into each category: fruits, grains, vegetables, protein, and dairy. If necessary, use a dictionary.
3. If possible, it's a good idea to talk to a nutritionist to check if you're categorizing the foods correctly.

Draft

4. Make your weekly menu planner: divide a sheet of paper into the 7 days of the week and separate each day into 3 meals (breakfast, lunch, and dinner). For each meal, write what foods and the quantity you're planning to eat.
5. Proofread your text.

Remember!

Be realistic! Don't include foods that are difficult to find where you live or that are too expensive. Healthy meals don't have to be exotic or expensive!

As you plan your menu, consider these tips:

Balancing Calories

- Enjoy your food, but eat less.
- Avoid oversized portions.

Foods to Increase

- Make half your plate fruits and vegetables.
- Make at least half your grains whole grains.
- Switch to fat-free or low-fat milk.

Foods to Reduce

- Compare sodium in foods like soup, bread, and frozen meals – and choose the foods with lower numbers.
- Drink water instead of sugary drinks.

Adapted from ChooseMyPlate.gov

Final version

6. Write the final version of your plan.

Share

7. Share your plan with your family. It's easier to follow a healthy diet when everyone in the family follows it too!

Go to *Looking Back* on page 73 ▶

Stopover Units 3 & 4

START

The Statute of the Child and Adolescent was passed on July 13, 1990.

You must be 14 years old to work.

go BACK 3 spaces

A child is a person that is twelve years old (completed).

Teachers don't have to respect children and adolescents in schools.

MISS a turn

Children and adolescents have the right to practice sports and have entertainment.

Children and adolescents are free to practice their religion.

Children and adolescents can buy products that don't cause physical damage in the case of improper use.

Children and adolescents have the right to discuss the criteria of an evaluation.

Children and adolescents have the right to live in community, without discrimination.

Children and adolescents can't participate in political life.

go BACK 3 spaces

Some magazines can't be sold to children or adolescents.

END

Play this game and learn more about your rights and obligations.

- Use a dice to move. Say if the sentences are true or false. The other players will check if your answers are right or wrong. You can read the excerpts from the statute to help you.
- If your answer is incorrect, go back to the space you were on before.
- The winner is the first student to return to START.

Law nº 8,069, July 13, 1990

Treats of The Statute of the Child and Adolescent, and takes other measures.

THE PRESIDENT OF THE REPUBLIC

I hereby make it known that the National Congress decrees and I sanction the following Law:

BOOK I – GENERIC

TITLE I – PRELIMINARY PROVISIONS

Art. 2. For the purposes of this Law, the child is considered as the person who has not yet completed twelve years of age and the adolescent as that between twelve and eighteen years of age.

⋮

TITLE II – FUNDAMENTAL RIGHTS

CHAPTER I – THE RIGHT OF LIFE AND HEALTH

Art. 14. The Unified System of Health will promote programs of medical and dental assistance for prevention of the infirmities that normally affect the young population, together with campaigns of health education for parents, educators, and students.

Paragraph. In the cases recommended by health authorities, vaccination of children is obligatory.

⋮

CHAPTER II – THE RIGHT TO FREEDOM, RESPECT AND DIGNITY

Art. 16. The right to freedom encompasses the following aspects:

I – going, coming and remaining in public places and community spaces, except as determined by legal restrictions;

Board game: The Statute of the Child and Adolescent

MISS a turn

Some vaccines for children are an obligation.

Children must have free access to school.

Children can buy lottery tickets.

ADVANCE 2 spaces

An adolescent is a person that is between 14 and 18 years old (completed)

The Unified System of Health must provide medical assistance for children.

MISS a turn

Children and adolescents shouldn't live with people dependent on narcotic substances.

All children and adolescents must have the same conditions for access and permanence in school.

Only adolescents can have access to alcoholic drinks.

go BACK 3 spaces

You can work as an apprentice if you are 13 years of age.

ADVANCE 2 spaces

Adolescents can buy fireworks.

go BACK 3 spaces

II – opinion and expression;
III – belief and religious practice;
IV – play, sports practice, and entertainment;
V – participation in family and community life, without discrimination;
VI – participation in political life, according to the terms of the law;
VII – seeking refuge, aid, and guidance.

⋮

CHAPTER III – THE RIGHT TO FAMILY AND COMMUNITY LIFE

Section I – General Provisions

Art. 19. Every child or adolescent has the right to be raised and educated in the midst of his family and, exceptionally, in a foster family, in such a way as to ensure family and community life in an environment free of the presence of persons dependent on narcotic substances.

⋮

CHAPTER IV – THE RIGHT TO EDUCATION, CULTURE, SPORTS PRACTICE AND LEISURE

Art. 53. The child and adolescent have the right to education, with the objective of the full development of their person, preparation for the exercise of citizenship and qualification for work, and they are ensured of the following:
I – equality of conditions for access and permanence in school;
II – the right to be respected by their educators;
III – the right to contest criteria of evaluation, together with the right to appeal to higher educational jurisdiction;
IV – the right to organize and participate in student entities;
V – access to a public school near his residence and free of charge.

⋮

CHAPTER V – THE RIGHT TO VOCATIONAL TRAINING AND PROTECTION AT WORK

Art. 60. Work is prohibited to minors of less than fourteen years of age, except as apprentices.

⋮

CHAPTER II – SPECIAL PREVENTION

Section I – Information, Culture, Leisure, Sports, Entertainment and Shows

Section II – Products and Services

Art. 81. Sale of the following to children or adolescents is prohibited:
I – weapons, ammunition and explosives;
II – alcoholic beverages;
III – products containing ingredients that can cause physical or psychic dependence even when used improperly;
IV – fireworks and like products, except those which, due to their reduced potential, are incapable of causing physical damage in the case of improper use;
V – magazines and publications referred to in art. 78;
VI – lottery tickets and the like.

⋮

Brasilia, July 13, 1990; 169th Year of Independence and 102nd of the Republic.

Extra Reading 2

Leon Walter Tillage is an African American who lived in North Carolina in the 1940s. His autobiography named *Leon's Story* was the winner of the 1998 Boston Globe – Horn Book Award for Nonfiction. It's a personal history about discrimination, ethics, morality, historical social changes, and civil rights.

1 **Read an extract from the book and answer the questions that follow.**

AFTERWORD

I've worked anywhere you could work to get some money. The only decent job I've had is here in Baltimore; I've been a custodian at Park School going on thirty years. The rest of the jobs were just in and out, here and there. I did marry in North Carolina, but my wife and I divorced. We had a daughter, and she's still in Raleigh, where she's a nurse, doing good. I remarried and got separated, but I have two sons by that wife. My youngest son is in high school, and my oldest one, he went back down South.

I was honored because Park School where I work gave me a yearbook in my name, and a whole page, dedicated especially to me, and they had a big assembly. One of my brothers works here at the school, too, and the Alumni Council of Park School made a scholarship fund in our name honoring us for all our years at the school. The scholarship helps kids who live in Baltimore, whatever color they are.

The school gave a big party for my brother and me. They surprised us with a proclamation from the Maryland House of Delegates. It's very official. It declares the scholarship to be the law. Now, the proclamation certificate is up on the wall of the church where my mother is a deacon. She was the first woman deacon of the church. They have a parents-and-child corner there, and they put pictures up when anybody's kid is doing something good. They do that to try and influence the young people and try and help them see what some of the people are doing that come from that area. My brother and I, we're very proud of that.

Adapted from Amazon.com

Glossary

custodian: the professional who cleans and maintains a building.
nurse: a person trained to take care of people, usually in a hospital.
yearbook: a photo book of students who are graduating in a school or college with information about their school activities.
assembly: a group of people who get together in a place with a common objective.
scholarship: financial help to study.
deacon: someone whose job is to help a minister in some Protestant churches.

a Is he married?

....

b How many children does he have?

....

c Where does he work?

....

d How long has he worked there?

....

e Why did Leon's mother put the proclamation certificate on the wall of the church where she is a deacon?

....

....

2 Check the information that is implicit in the text.

- ◯ He has more than one brother.
- ◯ He didn't like his previous jobs.
- ◯ He doesn't talk to his sons anymore.
- ◯ Leon and his brother are good workers.
- ◯ The school asked the Maryland House of Delegates to recognize the scholarship.

3 The name of the chapter ("Afterword") means "a part at the end of a book that has a few final remarks". Why do you think the author decided to leave this information as final remarks?

....

....

....

....

....

Project 2

A picnic at school

1 Can you explain what the following concepts mean?

organic food **locally grown food**

seasonal fruits and vegetables

2 How often do you eat food that is organic, locally grown, and seasonal? Read some reasons to eat this type of food and answer: can you think of other reasons?

a By eating with the **seasons**, we are eating foods when they are the most abundant, the least expensive, and at their best in terms of taste.

b A dollar spent **locally** generates twice as much income for the local economy. When businesses are not owned locally, money leaves the community with every transaction.

c The food you buy in the supermarket has been refrigerated for days or weeks. The food you buy at your **local** farmer's market has often been picked within 24 hours of your purchase. This freshness affects the taste of your food and the nutritional value, which declines with time.

d Factory farms treat animals like products. They are kept in small confined places and often never move more than a few meters their whole lives. On **organic** farms, animals are raised without cruelty.

e By eating **organic**, you will dramatically reduce the amount of pesticide residue you ingest.

Adapted from PlanetGreen.Discovery.com

3 We are going to prepare a school picnic with organic, locally grown and seasonal food. First, find out what foods are in season. Then research and complete the chart.

Season we are in now:	
Fruits of the season	Vegetables of the season
....	....
....	....
....	....
....	....
....	....

4 **Find out what fruits, vegetables, or grains are cultivated where you live.**

I live in ....

Fruits, vegetables, or grains that are cultivated here:

....

....

5 **Where can you buy organic products in your city? Visit local markets that sell organic products and local farms that produce organic products and complete the chart.**

Where to buy	Product	Weight / quantity	Price

6 **Plan a picnic with your classmates.**

a Use the lists in **activities 3**, **4**, and **5** to plan the menu of the picnic using organic, locally grown, seasonal food. You can include other types of food that are not on your lists, but try to use the products as much as possible.

b What's the picnic budget? How much can each one of you contribute?

c Decide who is going to buy and prepare what. Also decide who is going to bring utensils: plates, napkins, glasses, tablecloth etc.

d Set a date and place to have the picnic. You can plan to have your picnic in a park, square, or open area near the school (check if these places require authorization for use). You could also have the picnic in the schoolyard!

e On the day of the picnic, talk about the experience of learning and researching about organic, locally grown, and seasonal food. How has this research changed the way you think about food?

f Have fun! A picnic is a great opportunity to have some quality time with your friends, enjoy the outdoors, and eat good food!

Think green!

- If possible, use reusable utensils (the ones you can wash and use again later). If not, buy recyclable or biodegradable ones.
- Buy foods without a lot of packaging and those that can be eaten without any utensils to minimize waste.
- Once your picnic is over, clean up everything and don't leave anything behind. Recyclable trash goes to special bins; if there aren't any available where you had the picnic, pack the trash and take it somewhere it can be properly disposed.

Looking Back at UNIT 1

Now I can...			Learn more about it:
read a review about a hotel.			Read other hotel reviews at <www.tripadvisor.com/ Hotels>.
talk about free time activities.			Read the story of a 13-year-old who spends his vacations trying to become a writer in the book *How I survived my summer vacation: and lived to write the Story*, by Robin Friedman.
use my leisure time to learn English.			
use the Simple Past and the correct pronunciation of verbs in the past to talk about a vacation.			Study the information on page 140 in the *Grammar Reference* section. Also, check <www.iesonava.info/olgaenlared/ edpronunciation.htm> for more information on how to pronounce the *–ed* in the regular verbs.
give opinions to talk about past events.			
read about vacations in the Northern Hemisphere to learn more about the seasons.			Watch an animation explaining about the weather on <www.edutube.org/video/what-causes-different-seasons-animation>.
listen to a testimonial about spending vacations at a summer camp.			
write a review to evaluate a place.			

Looking Back at UNIT 2

Now I can...			Learn more about it:
read a FAQ about memes.			Learn more about memes at <knowyourmeme.com>. Read the story of a boy who becomes famous at a school in *Alex King, famous fourth grader*, by Michele Hugelmeyer.
use the Simple Past to talk about memes and recent fads.			Study the information on page 141 in the *Grammar Reference* section.
use relaxed pronunciation in informal conversations.			
use *me too / me neither* to agree with a friend's opinion.			
describe fads and trends.			
read a text to understand the relation between genes and memes.			Watch the animations that explain about genetics and genes at <www.neok12.com/php/watch.php?v=zx57774078797d7564675a0a&t=Genetics>.
reflect on the influence of memes in your learning to identify what is more important and relevant to you			
listen to a conversation about the childhood of a group of friends.			
write a "Wanted" poster to make fun of a bad fad.			This type of poster appears frequently in movies, such as *Harry Potter and the prisoner of Azkaban* (2004).

Looking Back at UNIT 3

Now I can...			Learn more about it:
read campaign posters about discrimination.			Find other campaigns at <osocio.org/category/discrimination/>.
talk about prejudice.			Watch the movie *Pride* (2007), based on actual events that tells the story of an African-American swimmer who is a victim of racism.
understand other cultures to communicate better.			
practice the sounds of the letter *x* to pronounce some words appropriately.			To know more words with the letter *x*, go to <www.scrabblefinder.com/x-words-scrabble>.
read about The Universal Declaration of Human Rights to reflect about the situation in your country.			Find the complete declaration at <www.un.org>.
respond to senseless and irrational arguments.			
listen to a police dispatch call about crime.			
use *must*, *might*, *should*, and *might want to* to talk about tolerance and respect.			Study the information on page 142 in the *Grammar Reference* section.
write a campaign poster to protest.			

Looking Back at UNIT 4

Now I can...			Learn more about it:
read an article about how cookies are made.			Watch a video showing how cookies are made at <watch.discoverychannel.ca>. Learn about the specific legislation on the subject at <www.anvisa.gov.br>.
describe food.			Find other words to describe food at <www.macmillandictionary.com>.
listen to a dialog about Girl Scouts cookies.			
use expressions and emphasis to agree and disagree.			Find out more at <www.soundsofenglish.org>.
use the passive voice to talk about food.			Study the information on page 143 in the *Grammar Reference* section.
read an article about how food can affect your school performance.			Read more about the campaign *Feed me better* at <www.jamieoliver.com/school-dinners>.
develop the habit of drinking water to help you in your school performance.			
write a menu plan to help you follow a healthy diet.			Read *Chew on this: everything you don't want to know about fast food*, by Charles Wilson and Eric Schlosser and learn more about the fast food industry.

Review Units 1 to 4

1 **Derek and Will are talking about the weekend.**

- What did Derek do?

....

....

....

....

....

....

....

2 **Complete the table below with the past form of the verbs.**

Regular		Irregular	
Infinitive	Past	Infinitive	Past
enjoy	....	buy	....
learn	....	do	....
talk	....	get	....
walk	....	give	....
want	....	know	....
		read	....
		think	....

3 **Order this dialog.**

◯ Grandpa: Maybe you should help your mother sometimes. She might like some help.

◯ Grandpa: Well, things were different when I was a child. But I always helped her in the kitchen.

◯ Boy: Sexist?

◯ Grandpa: I loved cooking when I was a kid. But my father used to say that cooking was for women. He was a little sexist, you know.

◯ Grandpa: Yes, he didn't like to do things that he associated with women. Like cooking, cleaning the house… these activities were done by my mother.

◯ Grandpa: Grandma? I made these cookies!

◯ Boy: Did you use to help your mother when you were a child?

1 Boy: Hmm… I love when grandma makes these crumbly cookies.

◯ Boy: Really? I didn't know you knew how to cook.

◯ Boy: I never clean the house.

4 Write complete sentences using the passive voice and the words given.

a tamagotchi / invent / 1996

....

....

....

....

b platform boots / make / light materials

....

....

....

c saggy pants / sell / skateboard stores

....

....

....

d cell phone pendants / use / the 2000s

....

....

....

e terrariums / make / reptiles and plants

....

....

....

f hula hoop / invent / 1957

....

....

....

....

UNIT 5 Something to believe in

ITINERARY

In this unit, you will develop the following competences:

- Read an obituary to learn about a person's life;
- Learn words to talk about inspiration and motivation;
- Read a text to learn more about sign language;
- Listen to a motivational speech to get general and specific information;
- Use the Present Perfect to talk about something that happened in a period of time that is not finished;
- Use expressions to encourage and congratulate someone;
- Practice different intonations to express different feelings;
- Think about your attitudes to become better students;
- Write an obituary to reflect and think about the future you want to have.

Reading Obituary

1 **Who is an inspiration for you? Why?**

2 **How can you be an inspiration to other people?**

3 **An obituary is a story of a person's life that is published when the person dies. What do you know about obituaries?** GENRE

a What information is mentioned?

....

....

b Where are obituaries published?

....

c Which of the words / phrases below describe the ideal text of an obituary?

- ◯ Accurate.
- ◯ Repetitive.
- ◯ Interesting.
- ◯ Focus on the life, not on the death.
- ◯ Boring.
- ◯ Inspiring.
- ◯ Full description of the funeral.

d Why do you think people read obituaries?

....

....

....

4 **Read Mattie Stepanek's obituary and answer the questions.** SCAN

a Match.

1. peacemaker 2. wish 3. dystrophy 4. get through

- ◯ A condition in which a part of your body gradually becomes weaker.
- ◯ To survive a difficult situation.
- ◯ Someone who tries to end a war or to stop people from fighting.
- ◯ A desire or aspiration.

b Check all Mattie's accomplishments.

- ◯ He published 5 books.
- ◯ He wrote more than 2,000 poems.
- ◯ He appeared on TV.
- ◯ He recorded songs based on his poems.
- ◯ He became a peacemaker.
- ◯ He traveled around the world.
- ◯ He met his hero.
- ◯ He became an ambassador for the Muscular Dystrophy Association.

c Two concepts appeared constantly in Mattie's work and life: **heartsong** and **play after every storm**. Explain in your own words what they mean.

MATTIE STEPANEK

Poet, peacemaker, and inspiration

LOS ANGELES, CA
June 24, 2004

In the summer of 2001, doctors were so certain of Mattie's death that they asked him what his final wish was. He had three – to publish his book of poetry, to appear on Oprah Winfrey's television show as a spokesman for peace, and to meet his hero, former President Carter.

Mattie got all three wishes – and three more years of life in hearts of the nation. Mattie chatted with Carter by phone, appeared on "Oprah," and was named Muscular Dystrophy Association national goodwill ambassador. He told Winfrey after the Sept. 11 attacks that he wanted to be a peacemaker. In fact he became one of the show's favorite and Oprah Winfrey has called Mattie "an angel on Earth".

After that, he published five books of poetry, which together have sold more than 1.5 million copies – Heartsongs, Journey Through Heartsongs, Hope Through Heartsongs, Celebrate Through Heartsongs, and Loving Through Heartsongs. Last year, teen country singer Billy Gilman released an album, Music Through Heartsongs – Songs Based on the Poems of Mattie J. T. Stepanek.

Young Mattie started making poetry at age 3. His mother began writing down what he said until he could do it himself. Later, at the age of 4, he adopted the word "heartsong" and described it for interviewers as "your inner beauty, the song in your heart that wants you to help make yourself a better person, and to help other people do the same. Everybody has one." He wrote more than 2,000 poems, but "On Being a Champion," which describes overcoming challenges, was on his "top 10".

Mattie said he lived by three philosophies: his own (to play after every storm), his mother's (to celebrate life every day in some way), and Carter's (if you want something badly enough, never give up and you will succeed). "We all have life storms and when we recover from them, we should celebrate that we got through it. That's what my life's philosophy means: to remember to play after every storm." In a 2003 interview he said, "I'm not afraid of dying, I want to live and do as much as I can here on Earth."

Mattie died Tuesday at Children's National Medical Center in Washington of a rare form of muscular dystrophy. He was 13.

Adapted from Articles.LATimes.com

5 In the title of the obituary Mattie is called an "inspiration". Why? INFER

....

....

....

....

YOUR TAKE

Which of Mattie's three philosophies do you relate more to? Why?

....

....

Vocabulary Inspiration and motivation

1 **Read and match the words with their definition. Listen and check your work.** 23

We all have life storms and when we recover from them, we should celebrate that we **got through** it.
(Mattie Stepanek)

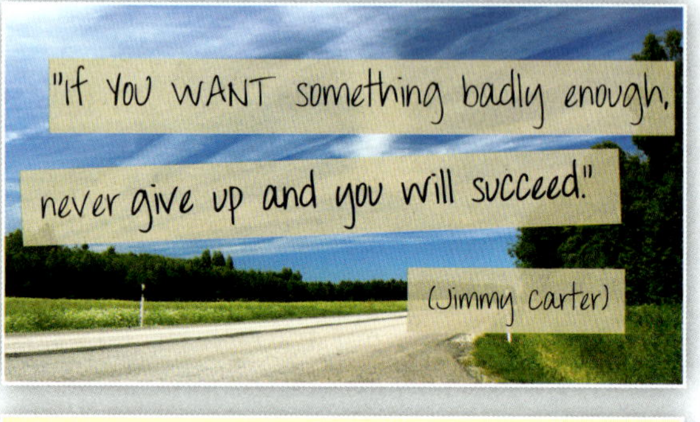

"Success isn't measured by the position you reach in life: it's measured by the obstacles you **overcome**."
(Booker T. Washington)

"WE CAN HAVE THE MOST DEDICATED TEACHERS, THE MOST SUPPORTIVE PARENTS, AND THE BEST SCHOOLS IN THE WORLD - AND NONE OF IT WILL MATTER IF YOU DON'T **FULFILL YOUR RESPONSIBILITIES**."

"IT'S YOUR PARENTS' RESPONSIBILITY TO MAKE SURE YOU **STAY ON TRACK**, AND YOU DO YOUR HOMEWORK, AND DON'T SPEND EVERY HOUR IN FRONT OF THE TV."

"YOU CAN'T DROP OUT OF SCHOOL AND JUST DROP INTO A GOOD JOB. YOU HAVE TO **WORK FOR IT** AND TRAIN FOR IT AND LEARN FOR IT."

(BARACK OBAMA)

a get through
b fulfill your responsibilities
c stay on track
d work for it
e give up
f overcome

( ) make an effort
( ) be victorious, conquer
(a) survive a difficult situation
( ) abandon
( ) continue in the correct way / trajectory
( ) complete / execute your obligations

2 **Complete the sentences with words or expressions from the activity 1.**

a We are almost in the end. Now is not time to ....!
b If you want to be the best, you have to ....
c My family had to .... very difficult times when we moved to Brazil.
d You have to .... many obstacles to be successful.
e Do you need some motivation to ....with your studying program?
f You can't .... if you don't know what they are.

3 **Which quotes above do you agree with? Which ones do you disagree with? Explain your reasons.**

....

....

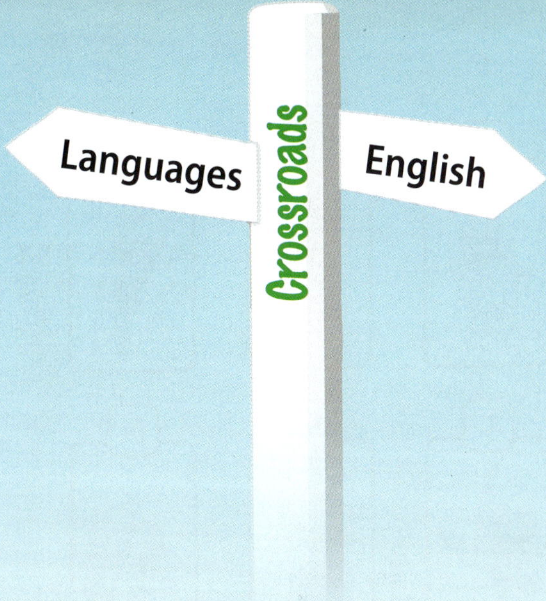

1 Being deaf or hard of hearing can't stop you from learning how to learn and speak a new language. Many people learn sign language in order to communicate with a hearing-impaired friend or loved one. What do you know about sign languages? Mark T (true) or F (false).

a ◯ You can express lots of words in sign language.
b ◯ You cannot express verb tenses (present, past, future) in sign language.
c ◯ The Brazilian sign language is called Libras.
d ◯ Sign languages are the same in all countries of the world.
e ◯ When you want to say your name in sign language, you have to spell it.

2 Can you say something in sign language? What?

3 Read the text about sign language and check your answers for activity 1.

Sign language

Sign languages are the means of communication of deaf communities. They are not simply mimics and gestures used by deaf people to facilitate communication. These are languages with grammatical structures and linguistic levels: the phonological, the morphological, the syntactic, and semantic. That also means that sign language speakers can produce very complex language like discuss philosophy, politics, and even produce poems and plays.

The *Libras*, the Brazilian sign language, has its origin in French sign language. Sign languages are not universal. Each country has its own sign language, which has the influence of the national culture. Like any other language, it also has expressions that differ from region to region (regionalism).

When you want to communicate something that has no specific gesture (your name, for example), you have to spell it.

Learn the alphabet in *Libras*.

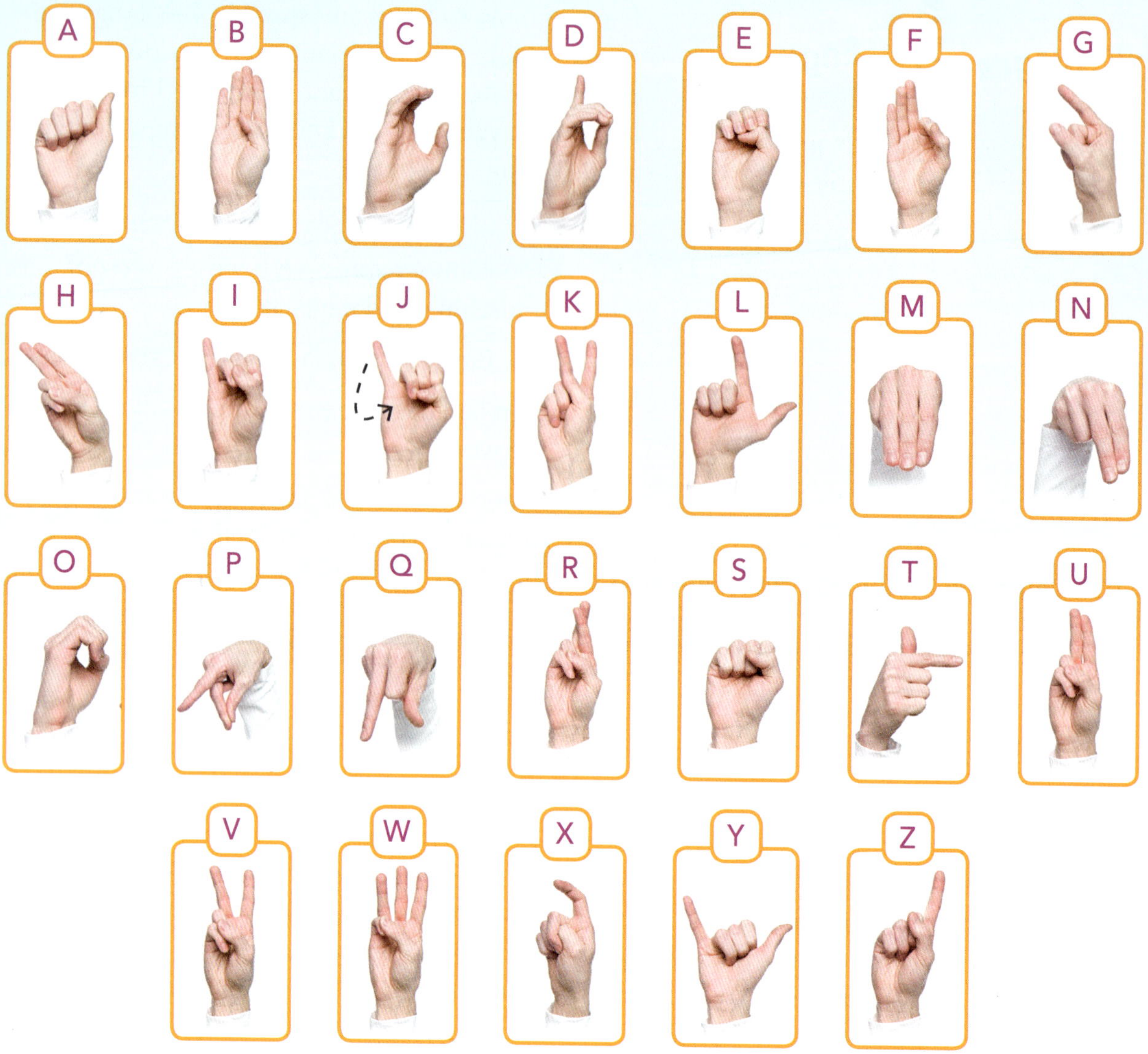

Adapted from Libras.org

REFLECT

1. Why is it important for deaf people to be able to use a language?
2. Why should people who are not deaf also learn *Libras*?

BY THE WAY...

Besides *Libras*, Brazil has another sign language called Urubú (also known as Urubú–Kaapor or Kaapor Sign Language). The Urubú sign language is used by the small community of Ka'apor people in the state of Maranhão. This community has a high ratio of deafness: 1 child in every 75 is born deaf. An interesting aspect of this language is that it locates the past in front of the speaker and the future, behind.

167

Listening Motivational speech

A **motivational speech** is a form of communication between a speaker and an audience with the objective to motivate the audience.

1 Many things are important when giving a motivational speech. GENRE Rank the items below in order of importance (1 – very important, 2 – important, 3 – not so important) according to your opinion. Explain.

- ◯ the use of gestures
- ◯ vocabulary
- ◯ humor
- ◯ control and tone of the voice
- ◯ fluency
- ◯ develop a relationship with the audience

2 Listen to the American president Barack Obama and answer the questions. 24

a What's the objective of his speech?

- ◯ To encourage students to do homework.
- ◯ To encourage students to study.
- ◯ To encourage students to take responsibility for their education.

b What does the speaker expect the audience to do?

- ◯ Have supportive teachers.
- ◯ Set educational goals and commit to them.
- ◯ Choose a profession soon.

c What's the tone of the motivational speaker? GENRE

- ◯ Energetic.
- ◯ Relaxing.

d How does the tone of the speaker affects the audience?

- ◯ It makes the audience sad and nostalgic.
- ◯ It makes the audience feel connected with the speaker and pay more attention to what he is saying.

Grammar Present Perfect

1 Read the sentences below and complete them appropriately.

1. Oprah Winfrey **has called** Mattie "an angel on Earth."
2. He published five books of poetry, which together **have sold** more than 1.5 million copies.

a This verb tense is called the Present Perfect. It's formed by the auxiliary verb .... + the main verb in the past participle.

b We use the Present Perfect tense to talk about something that happened in a period of time that is not finished. In sentence number .... , the period of time that is not finished is "Oprah's life", and in sentence number .... it is "until now".

> - To form the **negative**, we use ***hasn't / haven't***: *I haven't traveled to another country.*
> - To form the **interrogative**, we change the order: *Have you traveled to another country?*
> - To give **short answers**, we say: *Yes, I have. / No, I haven't.*

2 Mark the periods of time that are possible to use with the Present Perfect. Why the other options are not possible? Justify your answer.

◯ Yesterday.	◯ In my life.	◯ Today.
◯ This week.	◯ When I was a kid.	◯ Until now.
◯ On my last birthday.	◯ In Mattie Stepanek's life.	◯ During the movie we saw.

3 Complete the dialogs with the Present Perfect of the verbs given.

a (read)

A: ....Have........ you ....read........ any of Mattie Stepanek's poems?

B: Yes, ...I have...... . ...I have read...... "On Being a Champion." It's very inspiring!

b (find)

A: .... Heloise .... the book on motivational speeches?

B: No, ... She's still looking for it.

c (finished/ do/ print – negative)

A: I'm happy! I .... all my homework and it's still 4 pm.

B: .... the research for the Geography teacher?

A: Oh, no I forgot! And .... the photographs either! Not so happy after all...

4 Write four sentences about things you *have* or *haven't done* in each period below. Write about: *today, this week, this year* and *your life*.

Today: I have talked to my best friend.

5 Ask your classmates if they *have* or *haven't done* the same things.

Have you talked to your best friend today?
Yes, I have / No, I haven't.

Speaking Encouraging and congratulating

1 Listen to the dialog and repeat the sentences. 25

Boy: I can't do it, dad... I want to give up!
Father: **Come on! You can do it!**
Mother: Try it one more time, honey.
Boy: Hey, I did it! I'm riding my bike!
Father: **Way to go**, son!
Mother: **Great job!**

Encouraging someone	Congratulating someone
Come on! You can do it! Do your best!	Way to go! Give me 5! Congrats! Great job!

2 Look at the pictures and match them with the situations.

- ◯ I can't do this exercise.
- ◯ I am too tired to play.
- ◯ We won the basketball tournament.
- ◯ I have a lot of housework to do.
- ◯ I won first place in a music composition contest.
- ◯ We graduated.
- ◯ I lost a lot of weight.
- ◯ I never hit a strike.

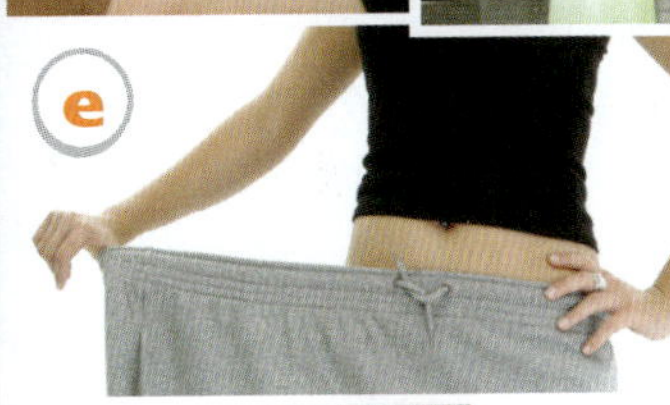

3 Imagine you are in one of those situations. In pairs, create a dialog using words of encouragement or congratulation. Use the expressions from the box.

Pronunciation Different intonation, different feelings

1 Listen and match. (26)

a Come on! ◯ encouraging someone

b Come on… ◯ impatient

c Come on! ◯ disagreeing with a behavior; a position, or an attitude

2 We use intonation to indicate the speaker's mood. Different intonation can transmit different feelings. Listen and write the mood each "come on" is expressing. (27)

Ceci: I can't decide on the shirt…
Gus: **Come on!** We are already late!

....

Paul: Eww… what's that in your hair?
Carol: **Come on**… stop it. It's not funny.

....

Player: I can't do it, coach. I'm too tired.
Coach: **Come on!** You can do it! Go back in there and do your best!

....

3 Listen again and repeat the three dialogs. Focus on expressing the different moods. (27)

↑ Road to success

Where there is a will, there's a way

A primeira atitude que precisamos desenvolver para nos tornar alunos bem-sucedidos é a motivação, principalmente a automotivação (aquela que vem de dentro de nós). Esperar que outra pessoa seja responsável pela nossa motivação é um erro que pode até levar à desmotivação no futuro. Quando estamos automotivados, nós nos esforçamos mais, buscamos novas maneiras de alcançar o sucesso e somos mais persistentes.

Identifique os motivos que fazem você perder a motivação e use essa informação em seu favor! Falta de confiança? Mantenha o pensamento positivo e um ritmo adequado, estude mais! Falta de foco? Aprenda a dar prioridade às coisas mais importantes, programe-se! Falta de direção? Converse com amigos, veja o progresso que alcançou, planeje o próximo passo e não deixe nenhuma tarefa inacabada.

Writing My own obituary

Writing your own obituary is an exercise of creating a character: yourself! What will they say about you in the newspaper? What did you do? What did you accomplish? How do you want to be remembered when you die?

Preparing to write

1. Read the characteristics of the genre **obituary** on page **78** again.
2. Read Mattie Stepanek's obituary again. What did he do? What did he accomplish? How is he remembered?
3. Reflect about your answers to the same questions.

Draft

4. Take your time and write the draft of your obituary.
5. Proofread your text.

Proofreading TIP

A **sequence connector** joins sentences and show the order of the ideas or events.

first, second, third...
before
after, then, later, next
finally

Examples:
... he wanted to be a peacemaker. **After** that, he published five books of poetry. **Later**, at the age of 4, he adopted the word "heartsong"...

Watch out!
We use *first*, *second*, *third*, *then*, *later*, *next* and *finally* followed by a comma. We use *before* and *after* followed by a complement: *before that*, *after that*, *before I go...*, *after she visited...*, etc.

Read your draft and answer these questions. Did you use sequence connectors? If not, why? Can you include these connectors and make your text more fluid?

Final version

6. Write the final version of your obituary.

Share

7. If you want, you can share your obituary with your classmates. If you don't want to, that's OK. Your obituary needs to inspire **yourself** so you can stay on track and reach your life goals.

Go to *Looking Back* on page 136 ▶

UNIT 6

Treat them right!

ITINERARY

In this unit, you will develop the following competences:

- reading newspaper headlines to get general and specific information about the treatment of animals;
- learning words to talk about farm animals, meat, and produce;
- practicing the sounds / ɪ / and / i / to pronounce some words appropriately;
- reading about Cesar Millan and learning more about being direct and consistent in your communication;
- reading a text and infograph to learn about sustainable development;
- listening to an opinion poll to get general and specific information about people's opinions on humanizing pets;
- using *going to* to talk about the future;
- learning expressions to start, support, answer, and conclude arguments in a debate;
- writing a petition to fight for a cause.

Reading Newspaper headlines

1 Look at the photos and read the captions. Match them with the topics below.

a Blitz getting a new "hairstyle".

b Rise in numbers of animals put to sleep.

c Animals in confinement have no space or natural light.

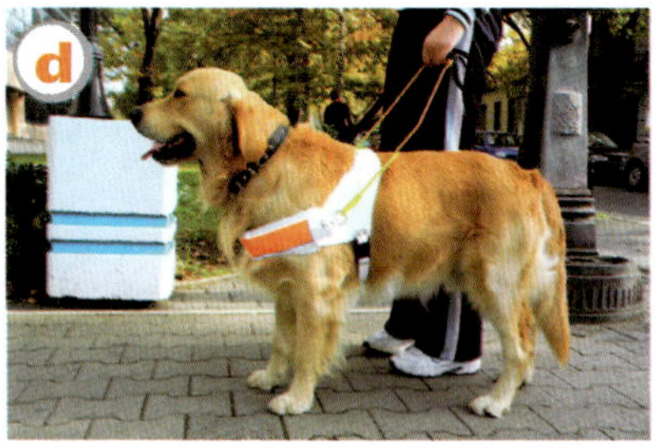

d The guide dog Tangerine on a street of Atlanta.

e Young boy holds a sign at the protest against animal abuse.

f Puppies rescued from facilities in poor conditions.

- (e) circus animals
- ( ) humanization of animals
- ( ) abandoned animals
- ( ) puppy mills
- ( ) inclusion of service animals in society
- ( ) confinement of farm animals

2 In your opinion, which photos show an ethical way of treating animals? Why?

....

3 A newspaper headline is a text at the top of an article. What do you know about headlines? Match the questions to the answers. GENRE

a What are the characteristics of a headline?

b What's the objective of a headline?

c Why are some headlines written with bigger letters than others?

d Why do people read headlines?

- ( ) The size of the headline depends on the article's importance: the most important story appears with a larger headline.
- ( ) It summarizes the story of the article. It's usually very short and economical in words. It can also be humorous or dramatic.
- ( ) Very few people read the entire newspaper. Usually we scan the newspaper and read the headlines before we choose what articles to read in detail.
- ( ) To call the reader's attention.

4 Read these newspaper headlines and match them with the pictures from activity 1. SKIM

○ **Animal Rights Group Protests Circus In Front Of School**
The circus is in town and the representatives from People for the Ethical Treatment of Animals, or PETA, are too. The group is protesting the treatment of circus elephants. The animal rights group was outside of Monte Sano Elementary School on Wednesday afternoon distributing pamphlets to families.

Adapted from WJBF.com

○ **130% rise in stray dogs put down by local authorities**
Last year 94 dogs were put to sleep while in 2011 the number has jumped to 217 in Scotland.

Adapted from News.STV.tv

○ **First dog grooming boutique opens in Germany**
A new dog boutique in Germany enables pet owners to give their pet a personal treatment comparable to that offered at the best luxury spas.

Adapted from DailyTimes.com.uk

○ **Humane Society takes in 12 dogs from puppy mill**
The Humane Society of North Iowa took in 12 dogs from a southern Iowa puppy mill this week through a coordinated rescue effort with the Animal Rescue League of Iowa.

Adapted from GlobeGazette.com

○ **Disabled woman awarded free service dog in Augusta**
Kelly Womack, from Augusta, Ga., will get a service dog for free. It takes about two years to train a service dog and it also costs about $ 20,000 dollars.

Adapted from WRDW.com

○ **Florida Introduces Bill to Ban Farm Animal Confinement**
Farm Sanctuary, the nation's leading farm animal protection organization, announces their support of a Florida bill, that allows certain farm animals the basic freedom of movement.

Adapted from WCTV.tv

5 Read the newspaper extracts and match the two parts of the sentences. SCAN

a The animal rights group protested against...
b The activists in Jakarta want to...
c A farm animal protection organization wants to...
d The Animal Rescue League of Iowa participated in...
e A service dog is given to...

○ ban farm animal confinement.
○ a disabled woman for free.
○ the treatment of circus elephants.
○ the rescue of dogs from puppy mills.
○ ban monkeys performing on the streets.

6 What are the possible reasons for the 130% rise in stray dogs put to sleep? INFER

....

....

7 What can we do to avoid animals in shelters being put to sleep?

....

....

Vocabulary Farm animals

1 Write the words from the box in the correct place. Then listen and check your answers. 28

horse • pig • lamb • eggs • piglet • chick • cow • chicken • beef • ham • duckling

	farm animals	young	meat	produce
	sheep	lamb	....	wool
	....	....	pork, bacon, ...	–
	hen (female) rooster (male)	....	....	....
	....	calf (singular) calves (plural)	....	milk, leather
	duck	....	duck	....
	....	foal	–	–

2 Complete Mateus' description of his last vacation.

Look at me in this photo feeding the ....! I took this photo on my last vacation when I went to my grandfather's farm in Indiana. I spent 10 days there. My grandfather taught me all about raising farm animals, and I even learned how to ride a ....! Every morning we woke up very early and collected the eggs that the .... and the .... laid. We also had to milk the .... before breakfast. He raises sheep too to produce the .... that makes the family's winter clothes. On my grandfather's farm the animals don't live in confinement; they all run free in a very big space. And it's very funny to see the .... play in the mud! I think I want to be a veterinarian and work with farm animals when I grow up!

3 Work in pairs. Answer the questions.

a Do you eat meat? What's your favorite kind of meat?
b How often do you eat lamb?
c Do you have clothes made with wool? What about leather?
d Do you (or anyone in your family) raise farm animals? Which ones?
e Considering the space you have in your house, would you like to have a farm animal as a pet? Which one?

Pronunciation

Pronunciation /i/ vs. /ɪ/

1 Listen and repeat. Notice the difference between the two sounds. 29

sheep /i/	pig /ɪ/

2 Listen and repeat the words with the same sound. 30

a beef – street – eat
b pig – milk – chicken – mill – piglet

Road to success

Be direct and consistent in your communication.

Cesar Millan, especialista em comportamento canino, diz que as lições mais valiosas que aprendeu vieram dos ensinamentos dos animais. Uma das lições que ele menciona é sobre comunicação: "Grandes relacionamentos, não importa a espécie, começam com uma comunicação clara e consistente. Essa é uma lição que devemos levar para outras áreas de nossas vidas, com nossa família, nossos amigos e nossos colegas de trabalho. Lembre-se: Nós ensinamos às pessoas a maneira como elas devem nos tratar."

Parade.com

Animal waste produced on large farms is a serious problem. Just to give you an idea of the problem, a single cow can produce about 50 kilos of waste per day. In the past, farmers would simply let the environment absorb this waste. Nowadays the production of meat, milk, and eggs has become more concentrated, and the correct management of farm waste is necessary to avoid environmental degradation. The solution to this problem should follow the concept of sustainable development.

1 **Sustainable development is development that doesn't damage the environment permanently and that considers the quality of life, not only for our generation, but for future generations too. Read the examples below and mark YES or NO.**

Action	**Is it a sustainable development action?**	
Using more gasoline and petroleum products.	◯ YES	◯ NO
Using alternative sources of energy.	◯ YES	◯ NO
A company planting trees to replace the trees that were extracted.	◯ YES	◯ NO
Building things that are energy efficient with renewable and recycled resources.	◯ YES	◯ NO
Eliminating green areas to build new houses.	◯ YES	◯ NO
Finding alternative ways to eliminate garbage and protect the environment.	◯ YES	◯ NO

2 **The infograph on page 95 explains how a biodigestor works. Look at it and check its benefits.**

- ◯ It generates renewable electricity.
- ◯ It reduces greenhouse gases (such as methane and carbon dioxide) produced by animal feces.
- ◯ It increases family income (selling extra electric energy).
- ◯ The use of feces protects the underground water from contamination.
- ◯ Gas can't be burned in winter to produce heat.
- ◯ Biodigestors reduce the bad smell.
- ◯ Biodigestors increase the presence of flies.
- ◯ You get a rich biofertilizer for free.
- ◯ Reduction of the use of artificial fertilizers.

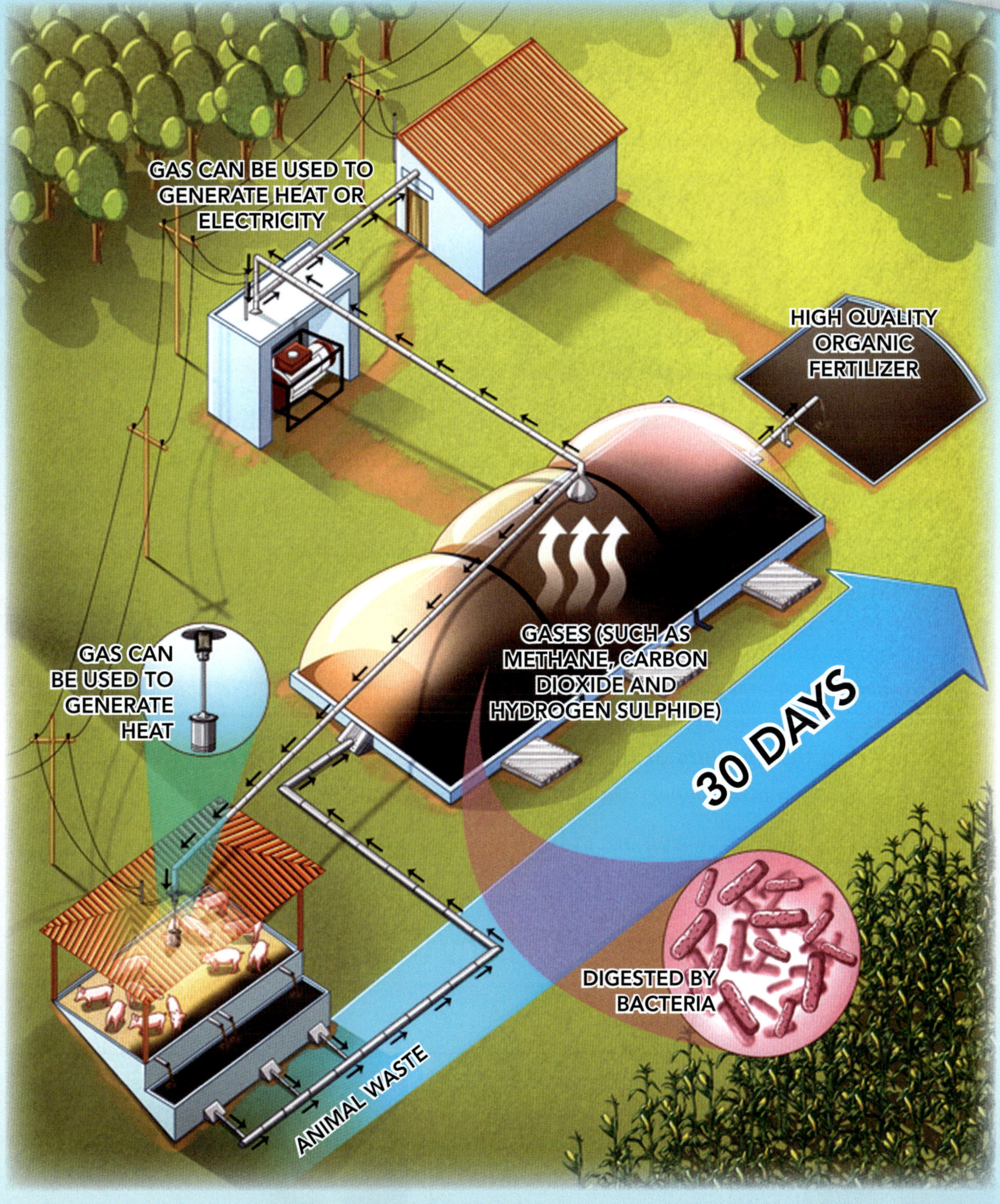

BY THE WAY...

If you have pets, you are responsible for the correct disposal of their waste.

- Don't leave it on the streets. Dog waste is a major cause of water pollution. It attracts flies, and the smell can disturb other people.
- Use biodegradable plastic bags or paper bags to collect your pet's waste. Regular plastic bags can take 100 years to decompose!
- Pet waste can be flushed down the toilet too. Use a scoop and throw it directly in the toilet.

Listening

167

An opinion poll

1 **An opinion poll is a public opinion survey to get information about a specific topic. Listen to the opinion poll, mark the photos related to the topic of the poll and answer: what's the poll about?** 31 SKIM

....

2 **Listen again and write down examples of how people humanize their pets.** 31 SCAN

....

....

....

3 **Considering the answers of the poll, which sentence is correct?**

◯ Most people interviewed are against humanizing pets.

◯ Most people interviewed are in favor of humanizing pets.

Grammar

Future with *going to*

1 **Read the examples and match.**

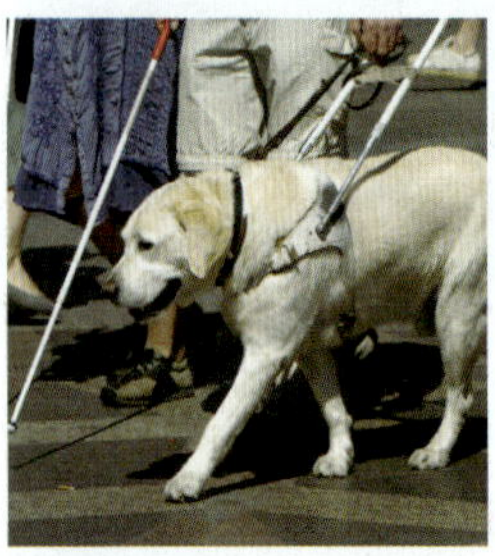

A: My service dog **is going to turn** 6 years old next month.
B: **Is** he **going to retire** soon?
A: No, not soon, he **isn't going to retire** before he is 7 years old.

A: What **is going to happen** to the circus monkeys?
B: They **are going to be returned** to the wild next week.

A: So you bought a pig farm! That's great! **Are you going to keep** the animals?
B: Of course! But **I'm not going to raise** my pigs in confinement! They **are not going to live** without the freedom to move about!

a In affirmative sentences, we use:

b In interrogative sentences, we use:

c In negative sentences, we use:

( ) subject + verb *to be* in the negative + *going to* + main verb

( ) subject + verb *to be* + *going to* + main verb

( ) verb *to be* + subject + *going to* + main verb

2 Read the news extracts and complete with the future *going to*.

treat • be • hand in • propose • require • start • wait

... the group .... a petition with 30 thousand signatures to the president, asking for the prohibition of animals in the circus. "The state senator .... the prohibition", said Jill Stewart, one of the activists.

Dog shelters expect the number of dogs put down to decrease with the new campaign. "We .... (negative) for the government to do something. We .... a campaign next week", said Mark Porter, co-founder of...

The dogs rescued from puppy mills .... (negative) available for adoption immediately. Veterinarians .... the animals first. "Since they spent their lives in cages, each dog .... house-training", said the Humane Society Director.

3 After all you learned in this unit, what are you going to change in your relationship with animals? Conduct an informal poll with your classmates.

You: Are you going to give chocolate to your dog?

Student A: No, I'm not.

Actions	Yes	No
Give chocolate to your dog.		
Buy dogs from puppy mills.		
Apply what you learned about sustainable development.		
Encourage people to adopt abandoned pets.		

Speaking Debate

1 Listen to this extract from a debate. 32

Thiago: **I'm against** parties for dogs **because** you shouldn't give cake and sweets to dogs; these things are not part of their diet. **Besides**, chocolate can kill a dog!

Renan: **I'm in favor**. I think dogs need to have fun too!

Thiago: **I see, but in fact** birthday parties are fun only for humans. **What I mean is**, dogs have fun in a different way.

Renan: **I understand your point, but the thing is** dogs have birthdays and we need to celebrate, right?

Thiago: **Yes, right but** a celebration for a dog is a different thing. **I'm convinced that** we can celebrate their birthdays without a party with cakes and sweets.

2 Read the examples.

To start your argument	To support your argument
I'm in favor of… because… I'm against… because…	Besides, What I mean is,
To answer to a contrary opinion	**To conclude your arguments**
I understand your point, but the thing is… I see, but in fact, Yes, right but	I'm convinced that… It's obvious that…

3 Work in pairs. Prepare for a debate.

a Choose one of the topics below and decide if you are in favor of or against it.
- Rodeos
- Manicures for dogs
- Having wild animals as pets (parrots, for example)

b Make a list of arguments to support your opinion.

c Make a list of arguments to support the contrary opinion.

d Rehearse a debate with your classmate.

e Get together with another classmate (who doesn't share the same opinion as you) and have a debate on the topic.

Attention!
- To answer to contrary arguments, you have to know what possible arguments there are.
- It's important to rehearse so that you make sure you are prepared.

Writing A petition

A **petition** is a document that is presented to an authority, usually containing signatures from many people, asking for action on a particular subject.

Preparing to write

1. Choose a cause for which you want to fight.
2. Considering the cause you chose, who should receive the petition?
3. Find out how many signatures you need for your petition to be accepted by the authorities.
4. Divide the page in 2 parts: the description of your cause at the top and four columns below for personal information (for example: name, email address, phone number, and signature).
5. Prepare a sufficient quantity of pages for the number of signatures that you need.

Draft

6. Write a short description of your cause. Include suggestions and reasons for your petition (for example: "We, students of White Hill School, petition the school principal to change the…").
7. Proofread your text.

Proofreading TIP

A good petition is concise and clear. The writing intends to first, persuade people to collaborate and sign. Then, to convince the authorities of the justice of your request. A good way to organize your petition is:

1. Describe the problem.
2. Suggest what is necessary to solve the problem.
3. Explain why it is necessary.

Read the first draft of your petition and check if your petition has all the three parts. If not, write what is missing. Then check if they are in the appropriate order.

You have learned before to revise your texts looking for problems in the sentences. This tip is to help you revise the organization of the complete text. Remember that the next time you write other texts!

Final version

8. Write a final version of your petition.

Share

9. Explain your cause and ask people to sign your petition.
10. When you have the necessary number of signatures, give the petition to the respective authority.

Stopover Units 5 & 6

1 Word ladder.

This word game was invented by Lewis Carroll, the author of *Alice in Wonderland*. See how to play:

- You have to change one word into another.
- At each step down, you can change **only one letter** to make a new word.
- At the end, you must have the final word.
- Read the clues for help.

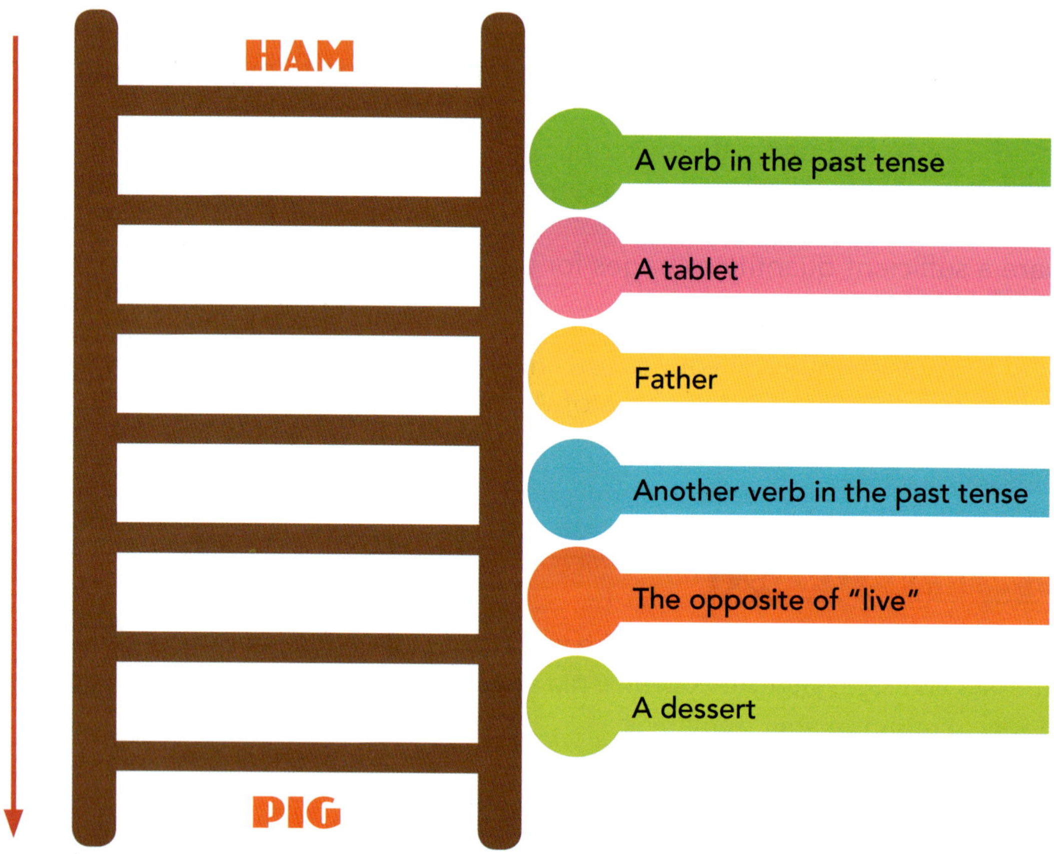

2 How many?

a Piglets? ....

b Lambs? ....

c Chicks? ....

d Calves? ....

e Ducklings? ....

f Foals? ....

3 Circle word games.

Find the hidden word in each circle. The word can start at any position, it can go from left to right or vice versa.

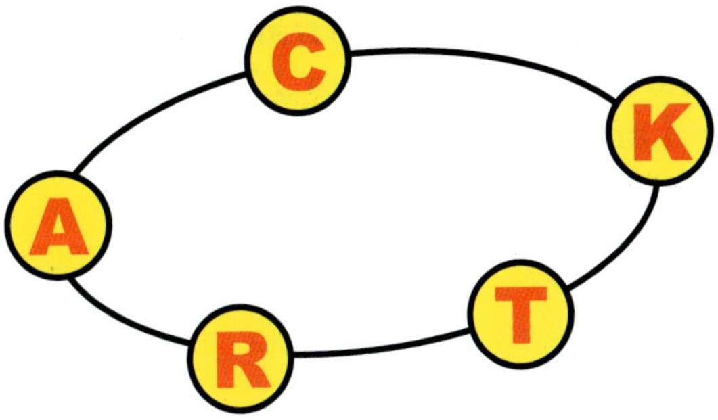

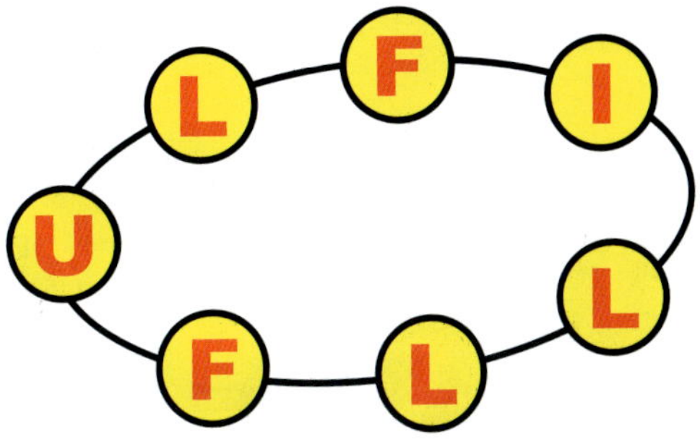

....

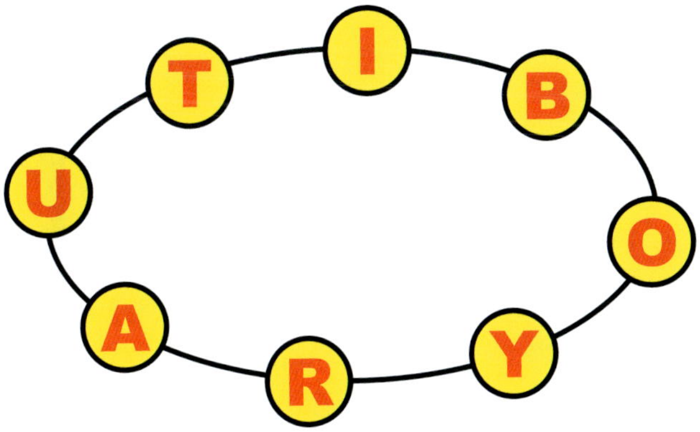

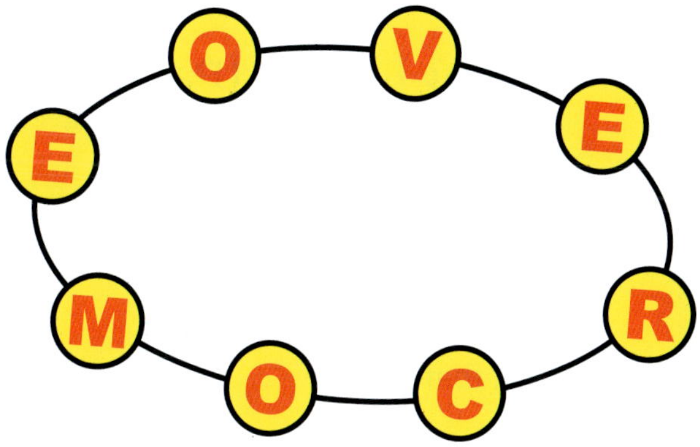

....

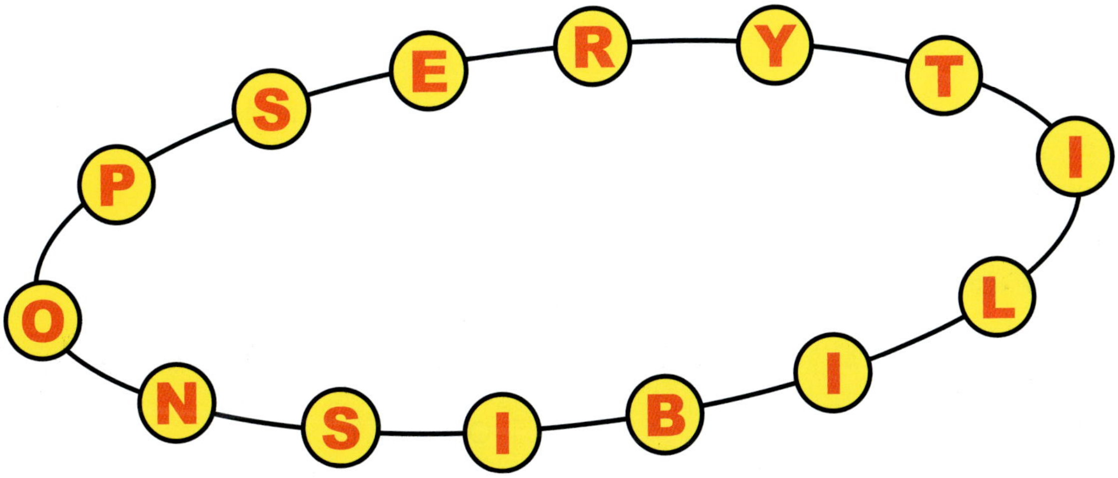

....

Extra Reading 3

Mattie and his service dog Micah.

1 **Read the poem from *Reflections of a Peacemaker: A Portrait Through Heartsongs* by Mattie J.T. Stepanek, and answer. What is the message of this poem?**

About Living (Part III)

I wanted to live
To be
One hundred and one
Years old.
But that is no
Longer my goal.
When I die,
I die.
I cannot predict.
I cannot control.
I cannot change
What is to be,
Which is what it is
And will be
What it will be.
I wanted to live
To be,
And not die.
But,
While I'm alive,
I live
To the fullest.
I treasure each sunrise.
I remember each sunset.
I dance every dance and
I sing every song and
I celebrate every moment.
I wanted to live
To be.
And,
I am spending my time
On earth before death
Living,
Rather than dying,
And not wasting a moment
Of the precious gifts
Of time and
Of life and
Of being, for now.

by Mattie J.T. Stepanek

Glossary

die: stop living; coming to death
alive: full of life
to the fullest: to the maximum
treasure: give importance; enjoy to the maximum
sunrise: the first light of day
sunset: the last light of day
rather than: in place of
wasting: using without objectives

2 Answer T (true) or F (false).

a ( ) He didn't want to live 100 years.
b ( ) He believes death is inevitable.
c ( ) He gives importance to many simple things.
d ( ) He wants to enjoy life while he can.

3 What do you understand by the underlined excerpt in the poem?

....

....

4 Poets often use language devices to evoke an emotional response from readers. Read about these two language devices.

- **Anaphora:** It consists of repeating a sequence of words at the beginning of neighboring clauses and it is used for emphasis.

  "Five years have passed;
  Five summers, with the length of
  Five long winters! and again I hear these waters..."
  (William Wordsworth, Tintern Abbey)

  "In every cry of every man,
  In every infant's cry of fear,
  In every voice, in every ban,
  The mind-forged manacles I hear:"
  (William Blake, London)

- **Tautophrase:** It is a phrase or sentence that repeats an idea in the same words and it is usually used for evasion. Examples:

  "A man's gotta do what a man's gotta do." (John Wayne)
  "If you want to fix the text, fix the text." (John R. Bolton)
  "A rose is a rose is a rose." (Gertrude Stein)

5 Find examples of anaphoras and tautophrases in Mattie's poem.

....

....

....

....

Project 3

Make a difference

1 **Read the text and answer: What do Jonas Rosa and Mattie Stepanek (from Unit 5, pages 78 / 79) have in common?**

Jonas Tadeu dos Santos Rosa is 15 years old and lives in a poor neighborhood of the city of São Paulo. Everyday he wakes up at 4:30 a.m. to go to school. He takes the train, the bus, and the subway to arrive at 7 a.m. at the private school he goes to, where he got a scholarship because of his excellent grades. During these long hours on public transportation, he noticed that deaf people had a lot of difficulties in asking for information in trains, subway stations, and bus stops. He decided to write a bill* for the implementation of a training course on *Libras* for public employees who work in areas with a great number of people in transit, such as train and subway stations. Because of his idea, he was selected to become a *Vereador Mirim* in the *Parlamento Jovem* of São Paulo. Now he can defend his bill, which can become a law in the future and positively change the life of many deaf people.

Translated and adapted from Camara.sp.gov.br

* A bill is a proposed law under consideration by a legislature. A bill becomes law after it is passed by the legislature and, in most cases, approved by the executive.

2 **Jonas decided to make a difference and fight for a cause after he experienced something in his community that opened his eyes to a problem.**
What are the problems of your community? Interview people who live and work in your community and make a list of problems and their possible causes and consequences.

Problem	Cause(s)	Consequences
There are lots of dogs and cats in the streets.	• People abandon their pets. • People don't neuter their pets.	• Lots of animals die of starvation or diseases. • Animals suffer violence and abuse. • Animals reproduce fast and the population of animals in the streets grows.
....	....	....

3 **Choose a problem from your list. What needs to be done to change this situation?**

....

....

4 **Research before you act.**

a Are there existing laws related to this situation? If so, who's responsible for checking the compliance with this law?

....

....

b Are there any NGOs working towards a solution? If so, what have they done?

....

....

c Are there volunteer programs acting on behalf of the cause? If so, how?

....

....

5 **What can you do about it? Choose one (or more) and complete.**

- ◯ We can start a project to ....
- ◯ We can do volunteer work at ....
- ◯ We can write a bill proposing ....

6 **What do you need before you do what you have to do: investments? equipment? Get organized! Ask your teachers, family, and friends for help.**

7 **Think about the results you want to reach with your actions. They are your target, so keep them in mind at all times.**

8 **Go ahead and do what you need to do!**

If you decide to...

- **start a project, make a video (in English) about your project and post it online.** Share your video with friends and family; send it to local TV / radio stations and international NGOs that fight for the same cause.
- **do volunteer work, work hard and keep a record (in English) of the process (you can take photos, make a journal, etc.).** Invite other people to join you. Look for online forums and communities of volunteers and share your experience. In the future, you can participate in the <www.escolavoluntaria.com.br/>.
- **write a bill, send it to a member of the legislative body of your city.** Make sure you send copies to other local authorities and influential people. Keep track of your bill and make sure it's not forgotten. Make a copy of your bill in English too, and send it to international NGOs that fight for the same cause.

9 **How can you inspire other people to make a difference too?**

UNIT 7 What the future holds

ITINERARY

In this unit, you will develop the following competences:

- reading quotations to get general and specific information about future predictions;
- using *will* and the correct pronunciation of its contraction to talk about the future;
- learning time expressions to talk about the future;
- reflecting on your mistakes to avoid repeating them in the future;
- using expressions to discuss predictions about the future;
- listening to a song to get general and specific information about how the singer feels about the future;
- reading a text about Easter Island to reflect on how history can teach us to avoid repeating the same mistakes;
- writing predictions about the future to publish on a website.

Reading Quotations

1 Read the definition below. Then find the underlined elements of a quotation in the example given. GENRE

A **quotation** consists of someone else's words that you mention when you are speaking or writing. The objective of a quotation is to inform the reader / listener of something.
It reflects the original source's opinion and can be used to exemplify or illustrate a topic. A quotation is punctuated with quotation marks and is attributed by reference to its original source.

> "*In the future everyone will be famous for fifteen minutes.*"
>
> (Andy Warhol, American painter and moviemaker, 1928-1987)

a Someone else: ....

b Topic: ....

c Quotation marks: ....

d Reference: ....

....

2 Read the quotations below and answer: what topic do the quotations best illustrate? SKIM

- ◯ Predictions that came true.
- ◯ Predictions that never came true.
- ◯ Predictions for the near future.

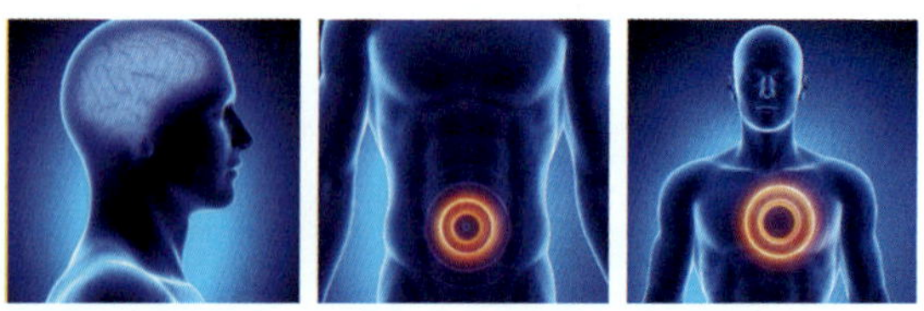

"The abdomen, the chest, and the brain will forever be shut from the intrusion of the wise and humane surgeon."
(John Eric Ericksen, British surgeon, to Queen Victoria, 1873)

"Heavier-than-air flying machines are impossible."
(Lord Kelvin, British mathematician and physicist, president of the British Royal Society, 1895)

"It doesn't matter what he does, he will never amount to anything."
(A teacher talking to Albert Einstein's father, 1895)

"Television won't last because people will soon get tired of staring at a plywood box every night."
(Darryl Zanuck, movie producer, 20th Century Fox, 1946)

"Nuclear-powered vacuum cleaners will probably be a reality in 10 years."
(Alex Lewyt, president of vacuum cleaner company Lewyt Corp., in *The New York Times* in 1955)

"Transmission of documents via telephone wires is possible in principle, but the apparatus required is so expensive that it will never become a practical proposition."
(Dennis Gabor, British physicist, 1962)

"[By 1985], machines [computers] will be capable of doing any work man can do."
(Herbert A. Simon, of Carnegie Mellon University, one of the founders of the field of artificial intelligence, speaking in 1965)

"[In Brazil] Football (soccer) will not catch on, you can be sure of it."
(Graciliano Ramos, Brazilian writer, 1921)

"It will be years – not in my time – before a woman will become Prime Minister."
(Margaret Thatcher, future Prime Minister, October 26th, 1969)

"It will be gone by June."
(*Variety* magazine, about rock'n' roll in 1955)

3 According to the quotations, which of these items didn't have a promising future?

SCAN

a ◯ cars
b ◯ brain surgery
c ◯ washing machines
d ◯ the airplane
e ◯ the TV
f ◯ rock 'n' roll
g ◯ nuclear power
h ◯ football (soccer)
i ◯ women in politics
j ◯ vacuum cleaners
k ◯ Albert Einstein

4 Match the columns.

a amount to	◯ become popular
b catch on	◯ application
c be gone	◯ necessary
d proposition	◯ intelligent
e required	◯ become
f shut	◯ disappear
g wise	◯ closed

5 Who made a wrong prediction about his / her own future?

....

6 There are two quotations that date very closely but express completely opposite opinions about what a certain machine would be able to do in the future. What are they? Why are they opposite?

....
....
....
....
....

YOUR TAKE

Why is it easy to make mistakes when we predict the future?

....

Grammar Future with *will*

1 We use *will* to make predictions about the future. Read the examples below and complete them with the words from the box.

Attention!
'll is the contraction of **will**
won't is the contraction of **will not**

subject • *will* • *not* • verb

A: Will television last?

B: Television won't last because people will get tired of staring at a plywood box every night.

a In affirmative sentences, we use .... + ... + ...

b In negative sentences, we use .... + ... + ...

c In interrogative sentences, we use .... + ... + ...

2 Complete this dialog appropriately using the verbs in parentheses, in the affirmative, negative or interrogative.

Sarah? Hi, it's me, Margareth. I don't think the rain .... (**stop**) soon. I think we .... (**have**) to cancel our picnic... Yes, I know... Oh, Monica and Dennis .... (**be**) happy, they were very excited about the picnic... yes... What? Tomorrow? I don't think the weather .... (**change**) tomorrow. And we .... (**be**) able to do it next weekend either, because Dennis .... probably .... (**be**) out of town. Oh, really? .... you .... (**travel**) to Los Angeles again? OK. Let me call them and see what we can do. Bye.

3 What will happen next? Complete the questions with the future with *will* and answer them.

a How ....will he get.... home? (get)
A mechanic will fix his car.

b What .... ? (find)

....

....

c What .... ? (say)

....

....

d .... ? (cry)

....

....

e What .... for dessert? (order)

....

....

Pronunciation Contraction of *will*

1 Listen and repeat. 33

I will - I'll
you will – you'll
he will – he'll
she will – she'll
we will – we'll
they will – they'll

167

2 Listen and repeat these sentences. Pay attention to the contracted form of *will*. 34

I'll have to study harder.
You'll be very happy with the news.
He'll arrive late again.
She'll be here in a minute.
We'll feel better tomorrow.
They'll be popular someday.

Vocabulary Time expressions used in the future

1 Listen and read the sentences. Then circle the words that indicate the time when something will happen. (35)

a I don't understand this problem. I will not finish tonight. I will talk to the teacher tomorrow.

b I believe she'll be back home in 2 hours. Will she find you at this number if she calls back later?

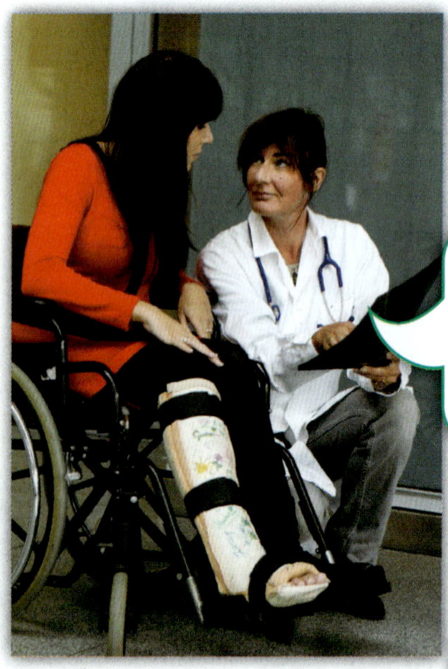

c We will probably take the cast off in two days, so you can start physical therapy next week.

d We won't receive these parts today, probably only the day after tomorrow, but it will be too late.

2 **Use the words and expressions from activity 1 to write sentences about the topics below.**

a The result of a soccer game or tournament.
b The events of a soap opera on TV.
c The weather for the weekend.
d The grades on a future test.

I think Corinthians will be the leader next week.
André will get an A in the math test tomorrow.

Road to success

Learn from your mistakes

Ninguém gosta de cometer erros, mas eles fazem parte do nosso desenvolvimento. Quando aprendemos algo, não absorvemos as informações e imediatamente as entendemos ou sabemos como usá-las. Precisamos testar, arriscar, praticar. Portanto, sempre existe a possibilidade de errarmos, assim como existe a oportunidade de aprendermos alguma coisa com os nossos erros. Identifique o que causou o erro, pense no que você aprendeu com ele e no que pode fazer para não repeti-lo no futuro.

Speaking Discussing predictions about the future

1 **Read the examples below.** 36

A: Will scientists find a cure for cancer?
B: **Yes, absolutely!** I'm sure they can do it.

A: Will there be wars in the future?
B: **Hmm... probably.** But our generation can stop that.

Yes, absolutely!

No, definitely not!

To express certainty

Hmm... probably.

Yes, maybe.

That's possible.

To express possibility

I really don't know.

Only time will tell.

To express lack of opinion

2 **Discuss your predictions about the future and explain your opinions. Use the expressions and the topics below.**

- People live underwater
- Paper books disappear
- PEOPLE HAVE BIONIC PARTS IN OUR BODIES
- OUR COUNTRY BECOME AN ECONOMIC POWER
- WE LIVE MORE THAN 130 YEARS
- the chinese language replace the english language in businesses
- Computers replace teachers in schools
- Make up your own: ....

Listening Song

1 **A song is a piece of music with words that you sing. What do you know about songs? Read the paragraph and complete it with the words from the box.** GENRE

chorus • lyrics • bridge • verses

The most important elements of a song are the .... and the .... Each verse usually has the same melody (possibly with some small modifications), but the .... change for most verses. In the chorus, lyrics are usually repeated. Pop songs that use verses and choruses often have a ...., which is a section that connects the verse and chorus at one or more points in the song.

2 **You are going to listen to a song called "Que Sera, Sera". What do you think the song is about?**

3 **Listen to the song and answer.** 37

a Check your predictions. What is the song about? SKIM

....

b Order the verses of the chorus.

- (1) Que sera, sera.
- ( ) What will be, will be.
- ( ) Que sera, sera.
- ( ) The future's not ours to see.
- ( ) Whatever will be, will be.

4 **The song is divided in 3 sections. In section 1, the singer talks about when she was just a little girl; in section 2, the singer talks about when she grew up and fell in love; in section 3, the singer talks about now she has children of her own.**

Listen to the song again and do what is asked. 37 SCAN

a Match the questions she asks in the song with sections **1** or **2**.

- ( ) What lies ahead?
- ( ) Will I be pretty?
- ( ) Will I be rich?
- ( ) Will we have rainbows day after day?
- ( ) What will I be?

b What questions do her children ask her in section **3**?

....

5 **Why are the questions in section 3 the same as the ones in section 1?** INFER

....

....

....

YOUR TAKE

Do you agree with the singer when she says "The future's not ours to see"? Explain.

....

....

BY THE WAY...

The expression "Que sera, sera" is grammatically incorrect in Spanish. The phrase came from an archaic Italian expression "Che sarà sarà", which the composer Jay Livingston saw in a movie. The correct Spanish phrase would be "Lo que sea, será".

History | Crossroads | English

1 Read the quote and answer: How is it connected to the topic of this unit?

"Those who cannot remember the past are condemned to repeat it."
(George Santayana, philosopher, essayist, poet, and novelist)

2 Read about the history of Easter Island and match the images to the sentences.

Easter Island and lessons learned

Easter Island is located in the Polynesian Triangle in Chilean territory. It is famous for its statues, called *moai*, made by the Rapanui people. The island was found by Europeans on an Easter Sunday in 1722 consequently receiving its name. It was an isolated volcanic land with no trees, just the *moai* statues "guarding" the island. Scientists have discovered that, in the past, the small island was covered with trees and vegetation. But the population grew and cut down the trees for canoes, huts, heat, and opening spaces to grow food. As the trees were not replaced, they were ending. In the 1500s, the shortage of trees had drastic effects on the life of the population. People had to abandon their huts to live in caves and use the hut wood for heat. They couldn't build canoes or nets for fishing anymore. The soil began to dry up with no nutrients to grow crops. After 1600, Easter Island's society started to decline because of the environmental collapse. On April 5, 1772, there were about 2,000 to 3,000 inhabitants on the island. Two years later the British explorer James Cook reported the statues were neglected. From 1862 to 1867, the population suffered with slavery and health problems. By 1877, there were just 111 people living on Easter Island. Until the present day, the island's population has slowly recovered, but with more than 97% of the population dead or not living there anymore, much of the island's cultural knowledge has been lost.

Glossary

- **huts:** cabanas
- **heat:** aquecimento
- **nets:** redes
- **slavery:** escravidão

Adapted from MamaDragonfly2677.hubpages.com

a 

b 

( ) What Europeans saw when they arrived on Easter Island.

( ) How Easter Island was, according to scientists.

3 What caused the changes to the island's environment?

....

....

4 What were the consequences of those changes? ....

....

....

....

5 What lesson do we learn from the history of Easter Island?

....

....

Writing What the future holds

People are always fascinated by the future and the possibility of predicting what will happen. What if your predictions are right? You should document them for future generations!

Preparing to write

1. Decide on the topic for your predictions (weather, science, fashion, technology, food, houses, etc.).
2. Who will be interested in reading your predictions? Decide how to publish your predictions.
3. There are websites and online forums (for example, www.whatfutureholds.com/) where you can read collections of predictions to get inspired and avoid repeating what someone else has already predicted.

Draft

4. Write your predictions in clear and objective sentences.
   Remember: For people to be interested in your predictions, they have to be about something that people had never thought about. So be creative!
5. Proofread your text.

Proofreading TIP

Spelling mistakes are common when we write. Sometimes because we do not know the correct spelling, but sometimes because we are distracted. Another very common source of spelling mistakes are typos. This kind of mistake happens when you are typing fast on a computer and you do not notice that you changed the order of some letters in a word. A common case in English is to write "teh" instead of "the". Check out some tips to proofread your text and avoid spelling mistakes.

a. Start reading from the last word and continue in reverse order to the beginning. This is better because when we read a text in the right order, our mind "fills in the blanks" and sometimes reads words or letters that are not there. If you read out of order, your brain is not distracted with meaning and can see details like typos.

b. Read your text aloud. This helps you read the words one by one, so you have more chances to see small mistakes.

Final version

6. Write the final version of your predictions.

Share

7. Publish your predictions (according to what was decided in **item 2**). Make sure your classmates read your predictions.
8. Keep track of your predictions and when the time for them to come true arrives, you can check if you are a real visionary or not!

UNIT 8

Life is what you make of it

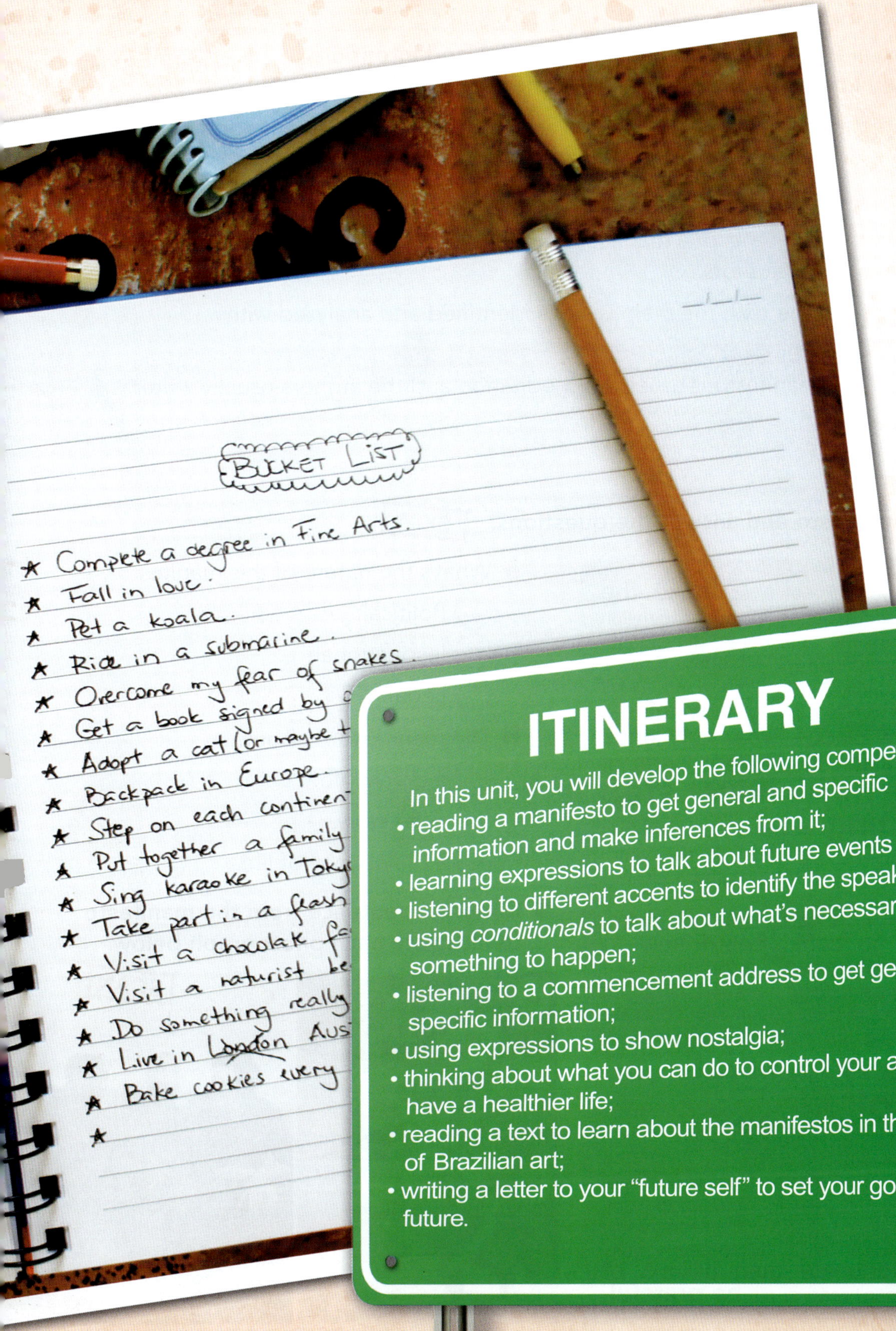

ITINERARY

In this unit, you will develop the following competences:

- reading a manifesto to get general and specific information and make inferences from it;
- learning expressions to talk about future events in your life;
- listening to different accents to identify the speaker's origin;
- using *conditionals* to talk about what's necessary for something to happen;
- listening to a commencement address to get general and specific information;
- using expressions to show nostalgia;
- thinking about what you can do to control your anxiety and have a healthier life;
- reading a text to learn about the manifestos in the history of Brazilian art;
- writing a letter to your "future self" to set your goals for the future.

Reading Manifesto

1 A manifesto is a public declaration of principles and intentions. What do you know about manifestos? Mark the correct sentences. GENRE

- ◯ The objective of a manifesto is to declare a certain point of view, report a problem, or demand the community take a certain action.
- ◯ The nature of a manifesto is always political.
- ◯ The essential elements of a manifesto are title, body of text, date, and signatures of the authors.
- ◯ In the body of the text, the main issue is identified and analyzed with solid arguments.
- ◯ The tone of a manifesto is usually of meditation and the authors usually write to themselves.

2 Read the manifesto and answer the questions. SKIM

Life is what you make of it, so **make the best of it**. Learn when to let your imagination fly and when to keep your feet on the ground. Believe that your dream will come true. There's a huge world outside your own world. Don't spend your life limiting it. **Try new things, travel to new places, wear new kinds of clothes, listen to different kinds of music**. Accept advice but **never stop questioning**; whenever someone tells you what you should or shouldn't do, ask "why". Take some time to learn how to grow your own food. Words are not always necessary; say less and do more. **Learn how to swim. Learn how to cook. Learn how to speak a foreign language.** And keep on learning; great opportunities will pass you by if you are not willing to learn new skills. Do not do something just because everyone else is doing it too. **Appreciate all forms of life**: humans, animals, plants, and any other that might come along; nature is all about balance. You are respected if you show respect. If you can't fully understand it, don't judge it. If you don't have good reasons to stay, leave. If you know something funny, share it. If you can read this message **you are more fortunate than billions of people** who can't read at all; **be grateful**.

a What's the nature of this manifesto?

- ◯ Political.
- ◯ Inspirational.
- ◯ Legal.

b The manifesto is about...

- ◯ a dream life.
- ◯ a life story.
- ◯ a philosophy of life.

3 Choose a sentence from the manifesto to illustrate each photograph below. SCAN

4 Why do you think some sentences use bigger letters than others? INFER

....

....

....

5 If the manifesto were spoken and not written, how would the words in the opening sentence be stressed? Why?

- ◯ LIFE is what you make of it. ....
- ◯ Life is what YOU make of it. ....
- ◯ Life is what you make of IT. ....

YOUR TAKE

What's your favorite sentence from the manifesto? Why?

....

....

Vocabulary What's next in your life?

1 Read and listen to five students from an international school talking about the future. Then, read the dialog, and organize the key phrases into the correct columns. 38

Kevin: I think I'll <u>go to a technical high school</u>, guys. I want to <u>get a part-time job</u> next year, <u>earn a salary</u>, <u>open a savings account</u>, and if I can't <u>get into a public university</u>, I can pay for a private university with my own money.

Paul: Wow! Great plans, man. Good for you! My family is going to <u>move to</u> Rio next year, so I really don't know what my future will be like…

Winnie: You're moving to Rio? I can't believe you're going to abandon us! I'm sad!

Cara: Oh, you will love Rio, Paul. The city is beautiful and you will <u>make new friends</u> there, I'm sure.

Paul: I know, It's a confusing feeling... sometimes I like the idea, sometimes I don't. I guess it's never easy to <u>start a new life</u> in a different city. But, don't worry, I'll <u>keep in touch with my old friends</u>!

Cara: I hope so! Well, as for my future, if my parents let me, I'll <u>apply for a scholarship</u> at a drama school. If they don't, I guess I'll <u>take</u> singing <u>classes</u> after school.

Paul: Do you guys ever think about the future, like, if you will get married, have children, and stuff?

Kevin, Cara, Winnie and Debbie: No! Hahahah.

Winnie: When I finish high school, I want to take some time off and travel the world before I start thinking about all these things.

Debbie: Guys, you know what? We should celebrate the end of 9th grade! Why don't we have a graduation party? That would be so cool!

Kevin: Great idea!

Education	Career and Money	Social Life	Leisure
....	....	....	....
....	....	....	....
....	....	....	....
....	....	....	....
....	....	....	....
....	....	....	....
....	....	....	....
....	....	....	....
....	....	....	....

2 Complete with the correct phrases from activity 1.

a If you don't have enough money to pay for your education, you can ....

b If you are not sure about what career to follow after university, maybe you should .... to think about the possibilities.

c Don't just complain if you are unhappy. Do something about it! There's always time to ....!

d You should .... It will certainly open your mind to new things; you will .... , see new places, and even discover a lot about yourself during the trip!

3 Work with a partner. Use the phrases from activity 1 in the questions. Give more details in your answers.

A: Do you plan to go to a technical high school?

B: Yes, I want to study interior design.

B: No, I want to study at a regular high school.

B: I'm not sure yet.

Pronunciation Same language, different accents

An **accent** is a characteristic pronunciation of a group of people of the same region, social and socio-economic class, ethnicity, or nationality.
English-speaking countries have their own distinguished accents.

1 Listen to the dialog on pages 121 / 122 again and answer. 38

a How many different accents are there? ....

b Who has the same accent? ....

2 Listen to these people from different nationalities saying the same sentence and answer the questions. 39

- I think the weather today is better for fishing.

a (English accent) What happens to the sound of the letter **r** in **weather** and **better**? ....

b (American accent) How does he pronounce the sound of **tt** in **better**?

....

c (Irish accent) How does he pronounce the sound of **th** in **think**?

....

d (Scottish accent) What happens to the sound of the letter **r** in **weather** and **better**? ....

e (Australian accent) How does he pronounce the sound of **ay** in **today**?

....

f (South African accent) Are the consonants pronounced clearly or softly? ....

167

Grammar Zero and first conditionals

We use **conditional sentences** to talk about certain conditions that are necessary for something to happen. A conditional sentence consists of two parts: a sentence with **if** (or *if-clause*) and a main clause.

a If there is no air, there is no fire.
if-clause / main clause

b If you don't like something, change it.
if-clause / main clause

c If you take this medicine, you will feel better.
if-clause / main clause

Examples **a** and **b** are also known as "zero conditionals".
Example **c** is also known as "first conditional".

1 **Read the examples again and complete the sentences appropriately.**

a The .... conditional is used to talk about the future.

b The .... conditional is used to talk about things that are always true (for example, scientific facts and general truths) or to give instructions and advice.

2 **Check the correct alternative.**

a What is the structure of zero conditional sentences?

◯ Verb in the present in the if-clause, **will** in the main clause.

◯ Verb in the present in the if-clause, verb in the present or the imperative in the main clause.

b What is the structure of first conditional sentences?

◯ Verb in the present in the if-clause, **will** in the main clause.

◯ Verb in the present in the if-clause, verb in the present or the imperative in the main clause.

3 **Look at the pictures and first parts of the sentences. Then match with the parts that complete them.**

a

If you like electronic music,

b

If you don't water plants,

c

If you arrive before seven,

d

If we follow the GPS,

◯ they will die.

◯ we will not get lost.

◯ you love this CD.

◯ they die.

(a) you will love this CD.

◯ you will wait for me.

◯ wait for me in front of the theater.

◯ we are lost.

4 **Answer the questions using the appropriate conditional sentence type.**

a Q: What do you do when you have personal problems?

A: If I have problems, ...

b Q: What will you do if you get a bad grade on the next test?

A: If I get a bad grade on the next test, ...

c Q: What do you do if you are bored?

A: If I am bored, ...

d Q: What will you study in the future if you have the chance?

A: If I have the chance, ...

5 **Talk to a classmate and discuss your options for the future (next weekend, next month, next year, when you finish high school, etc.). Give your classmate some advice.**

A: If the weather is good, I will travel to the beach next weekend.

B: If you go to Santos, visit the Museu do Surf; it's a great place.

Listening A commencement address

A commencement address is a speech given to students who are graduating. The objective of a commencement address is to be thought-provoking and inspire the students. The speakers are usually politicians, important citizens, or other notable figures in the community. The commencement address is delivered during the graduation ceremony.

1 **What do you think are common topics for commencement addresses?** GENRE

....

....

2 **Match the words with their meanings.**

a drop out
b calligraphy
c typography
d look forward
e look backwards
f connect the dots

( ) appearance of the words and letters.
( ) associate one idea with another to understand the complete context.
( ) think about the future.
( ) beautiful writing.
( ) think about the past.
( ) abandon (a course).

3 **You're going to listen to a commencement address given by Steve Jobs at the Stanford University graduation in 2005. Who was Steve Jobs?**

....

....

....

4 **Listen to the first part of the commencement address. What does Steve Jobs talk about?** 40 SKIM

( ) His creativity and imagination.
( ) How his decisions influenced his future.
( ) What people should do when they go to college.

6 Listen again and mark T (True) or F (False). Correct the false ones. 40 SCAN

- ◯ Steve Jobs graduated in computer sciences.
- ◯ When he started college, he was very sure about what he wanted to do with his life.
- ◯ He took calligraphy classes.
- ◯ The calligraphy course he took influenced the way he created computers.
- ◯ Only now, when he remembers his past, he understands the importance of his decisions.

7 Listen to the end of his commencement address and answer. 41

a Where did he read that advice? ....

b When was that? ....

c Was this message important for him? ....

8 He finishes his commencement address by giving the students a piece of advice: "Stay hungry. Stay foolish." What does that mean?

....

....

....

YOUR TAKE

About the time when Steve Jobs had to drop out of college, he said, "It was very scary at the time, but looking back it was one of the best decisions I ever made." Do you also feel scared when you have to make big decisions? How do you deal with that feeling?

....

....

Road to success

Controlling your anxiety

Ansiedade é uma mistura de apreensão, angústia, aflição, incerteza e medo, uma sensação que é normal e que todos experimentamos vez ou outra, principalmente quando nossas vidas passam por grandes mudanças ou por momentos importantes. Essa é a ansiedade normal. Entretanto, é importante prestar atenção a sinais de ansiedade e preocupações excessivas, que afetam sua saúde e sua vida cotidiana, que se prolonguem por muito tempo. Se não souber definir qual é o nível da sua ansiedade, vale a pena conversar com seus pais ou professores o quanto antes, para evitar que ela se torne um problema e comprometa sua qualidade de vida.

Speaking Feeling nostalgic

We "feel nostalgic" when we think about things, people, or situations of the past that have a happy association for us.

1 **Read the dialog below and notice the expressions to express nostalgia.**

Terry: **I'll never forget the time** we worked together for the school science fair!
Sue: Yes, those days were fun.
Mary: And **I'll always remember that day when** we had a surprise party for Mrs. Oliveira.
Anne: Oh, yeah! That was great!
Terry: **I'm going to miss** school and some teachers.
Sue: Me too. And **I'm going to miss** you guys...

Feeling nostalgic

- I'm going to miss the…
- I'll always remember that day when…
- I'll never forget the time…

2 **Make a list of memorable moments you and your classmates had this year (or in previous years).**

....

....

....

....

....

3 **Get together in groups of four students and talk about the moments using the expressions from the box.**
Do your classmates remember those moments too?

Arts | Crossroads | English

Manifestos in the history of Brazilian art

The "Week of Modern Art" was the most important artistic movement in Brazil. It was organized by Brazilian artists, writers, and composers who wanted to promote the ideas and concepts of a new generation. Many modern artists such as Mário de Andrade, Oswald de Andrade, Víctor Brecheret, Anita Malfatti, Menotti Del Pichia, Heitor Villa-Lobos, Tarsila do Amaral, Di Cavalcanti, and others got together at the *Theatro Municipal de São Paulo* in 1922 to present their works in the areas of painting, sculpture, music, poetry, and literature.

The beginning of modernism in Brazil is marked by manifestos: the *Manifesto da Poesia Pau-Brasil* (1924) by Oswald de Andrade; the *Manifesto Nhenguaçu Verde-Amarelo* (1926) by Plínio Salgado, Menotti Del Picchia, Guilherme de Almeida, and Cassiano Ricardo; the *Manifesto Regionalista* (1926) by Centro Regionalista do Nordeste; and the *Manifesto Antropófago* (1928) by Oswald de Andrade, which is considered the most radical of them.

The Abaporu

The Abaporu – from Tupi *aba* (man), *pora* (people) and *ú* (eat), "man that eats people" – is a painting by Tarsila do Amaral, painted in 1928 as a birthday gift to Oswald de Andrade, her husband at the time. Today it is the most valued Brazilian painting in the world. It was sold for US$1.5 million to an Argentinian collector in 1995. It's now on exhibit at the *Museo de Arte Latinoamericano de Buenos Aires* (MALBA), Argentina. The painting was Oswald de Andrade's inspiration to write the *Manifesto Antropófago*.

Abaporu. Tarsila do Amaral, 1928. Óleo sobre tela, c.i.d., 85 x 73 cm. Colección Costantini (Buenos Aires, Argentina) © Tarsila do Amaral Empreendimentos. Foto de Romulo Fialdini.

The Manifesto Antropófago

The *Manifesto Antropófago* was published in *Revista Antropofagia*, and it proposed that the imported culture (the European culture) be devoured and then used to create a truly Brazilian identity. The name of the manifesto comes from an indigenous belief: cannibals ate their enemy, assuming they were thus absorbing the enemy's qualities.

Anthropophagy
the same as cannibalism, the act of eating human flesh.

1 Read the text and put the events in the order they happened.

- ( ) The *Manifesto Antropófago* was published.
- ( ) The Week of Modern Art happened in São Paulo.
- ( ) *The Abaporu* was bought for US$ 1.5 million.
- ( ) Tarsila do Amaral painted *The Abaporu*.

2 Answer.

a What inspired Oswald de Andrade to write the *Manifesto Antropófago*?

....

....

....

b What was the message of the *Manifesto Antropófago*?

....

....

YOUR TAKE

Do you think the intentions of the Manifesto have been achieved, that is, that today we have a truly Brazilian culture and identity?

....

Writing A letter to my future me

As you come to the end of a stage in your life, it is only natural that you stop and reflect about everything you have done and everything you still want to do. It's time to assess your past achievements and set goals for your future.

To do that, you are going to write a letter to yourself in the future, telling yourself what it feels like to be you at this exact moment and what you anticipate for your coming years.

Preparing to write

1. Choose a time in the future when you want to receive your own letter. It can be anytime from one to three years in the future.
2. Think about your accomplishments and experiences of the last four years. Make a list of the most memorable / important ones.
3. Think about the changes you want to make in your life in the areas of health, friends, school, family, your English studies, etc. Write a complete list with your objectives for the coming year(s).

Draft

4. Turn your list of achievements / experiences into sentences. Give details about each item: say how these achievements / experiences have made you feel, how much has changed in your life because of them, etc.
5. Think about the steps you need to take to be successful. For example, to improve your grades, you can study with a friend, buy a book, and study 2 extra hours per week. The more specific you are about your plans, the better chances you have to achieve them. You can also set a time limit for each item. For example: October; before school vacation; by Christmas, etc.
6. Write a draft of your letter.

Proofreading

7. Proofread your letter carefully.

Final version

8. Write a final version of your letter on paper or on <FutureMe.org>.

Share

9. If you've prepared your letter on paper, fold your letter and put it in an envelope. Write the date when you will open the letter on the envelope. Leave it somewhere you can see it every day so you don't forget to open it. If you have written it on the <FutureMe.org website>, just send it to the website and they will send it back to you on the correct date.

Remember!

- Always date a letter.
- A letter has a greeting line. It usually starts with *Dear* ________. In this case, you can write *Dear future (your name)*, or *Dear future me.*
- A letter has a beginning, a middle, and an end. You can begin by talking about your present life, write a second paragraph about your past, and the last paragraph about your future.
- Use all the connectors you have learned – *and, so, because, first, second,* etc. – to make the reading more fluent and coherent.
- A letter has a closing line that depends on the level of formality between the writer and the reader. Since you are writing to yourself, use *Love, Take care*, or any other more informal farewell.

Stopover Units 7 & 8

1 Crosswords.

Across (→)

4. two days from now.

Down (↓)

1. 120 minutes from now.

2. the opposite of previous.

3. not now.

4. between this afternoon and tomorrow morning.

5. the day after today.

2 **Read the clues below. Then unscramble the words and copy the letters in the numbered boxes to find out the secret word.**

go to a ? school	take computer ?	open a ? account
get into a ? university	get a ? job	get ?
apply for a ?	earn a ?	

HIANETLCC __ __ __ __ __ __ __ __ __ (box 6 = 11, box 9 = 8)

LUCBIP __ __ __ __ __ __ (box 1 = 1, box 3 = 6)

CSRALPIHHSO __ __ __ __ __ __ __ __ __ __ __ (box 4 = 2)

SLSACSE __ __ __ __ __ __ __ (box 6 = 12, box 7 = 3)

PRTIATEM __ __ __ __ __ __ __ __ (box 4 = 10, box 6 = 5)

RYASAL __ __ __ __ __ __ (box 1 = 4)

NIGVASS __ __ __ __ __ __ __ (box 4 = 7, box 7 = 13)

RIDRAME __ __ __ __ __ __ __ (box 5 = 9)

Secret Word __ __ __ __ __ __ __ __ __ __ __ __ __ (1 2 3 4 5 6 7 8 9 10 11 12 13)

3 **Order these pieces and find out a quote about the future.**

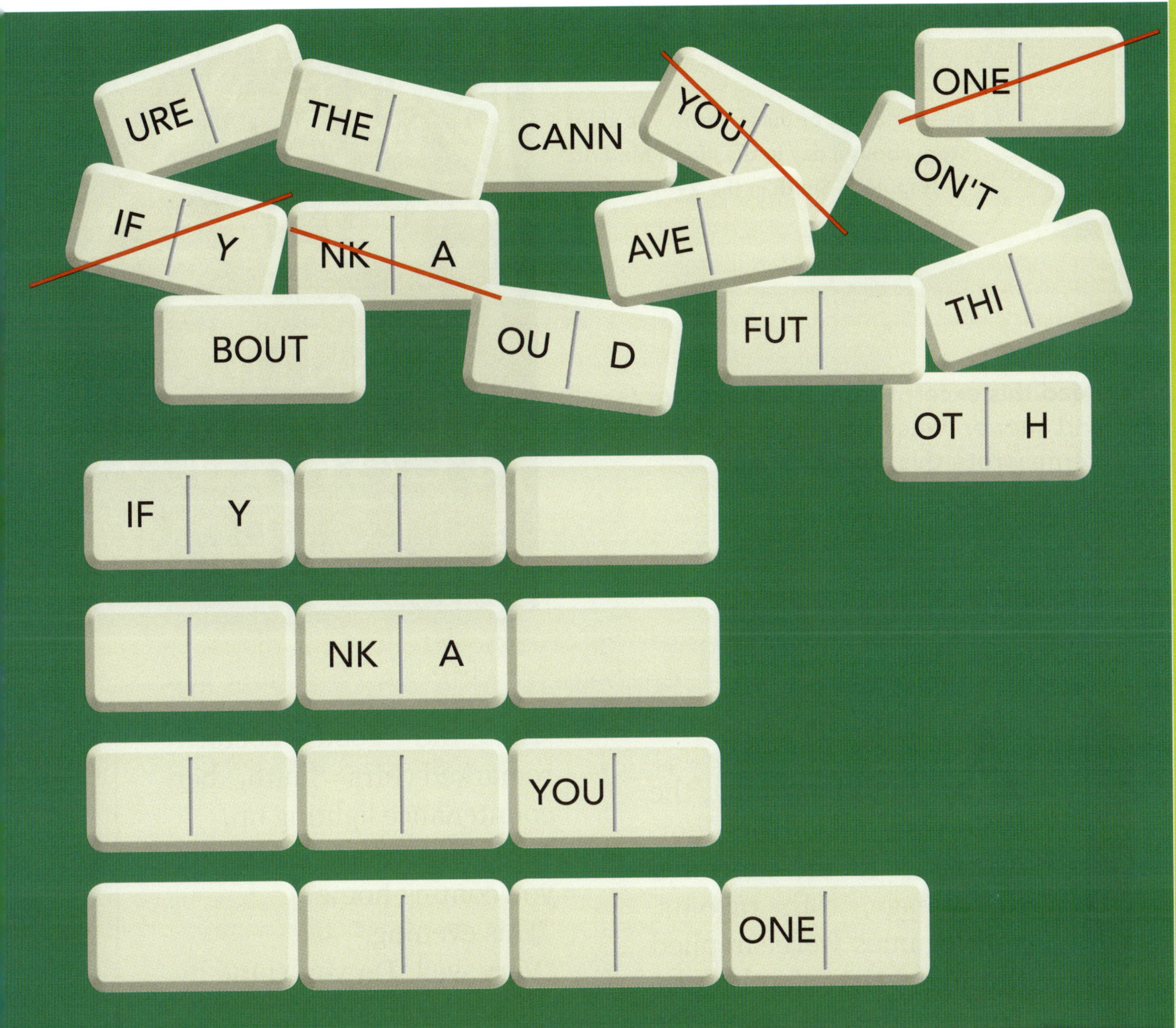

Quote: .... (John Golsworthy)

4 **Guessing game.**

a This word has 10 letters. If you take out 2, you get 18!

....

b When you have me, you want to share. If you share me, you will not have me. What am I?

....

c If you stop and look, you will always see me. If you try to touch me, you can't feel me. I can't move, but if you come to me, I will move away from you. What am I?

....

Extra Reading 4

In the year 2889, by Jules Verne, is a short story about a day in the life of Mr. Fritz Napoleon Smith in the 29th century.

1 Read this excerpt from the short story and answer: when do you think Jules Verne wrote this story?

a ◯ 1889.

b ◯ 1989.

c ◯ 1999.

As in the morning, the table rose out of the floor. Again, as in the morning, the potage, rôti, ragoûts, and legumes were supplied through the food-pipes. Toward the close of the meal, phonotelephotic communication was made with Paris. Smith saw his wife, seated alone at the dinner-table, looking anything but pleased at her loneliness.

"Pardon me, my dear, for having left you alone," he said through the telephone. "I was with Dr Wilkins."

"Ah, the good doctor!" remarked Mrs Smith, her countenance lighting up.

"Yes. But, pray, when are you coming home?"

"This evening."

"Very well. Do you come by tube or by air-train?"

"Oh, by tube."

"Yes; and at what hour will you arrive?"

"About eleven, I suppose."

"Eleven by Centropolis time, you mean?"

"Yes."

"Good-bye, then, for a little while," said Mr Smith as he severed communication with Paris.

Glossary

rose: past of rise; to appear, to come up
pipe: a duct or tubular structure
toward: in the direction of
loneliness: the state of having no company
countenance: face or facial expression

2 Read the extract again and answer.

a Is Mr Smith having breakfast?

....

....

b Mr Smith made "phonotelephotic communication" with Paris. What is the phonotelephote, in your opinion?

....

....

c Where is his wife?

....

....

d In your opinion, what are the tube and the air-train mentioned in the text?

....

....

....

3 The city of "Centropolis", mentioned in the text, is a famous city in the United States that will change its name in the future, according to Jules Verne's story. What is this city, in your opinion? Justify your answer. INFER

Jules Verne (1828-1905) was a French science-fiction author, considered the "Father of science fiction", famous for his novels *A Journey to the Centre of the Earth* (1864), *From the earth to the moon* (1865), *Twenty thousand leagues under the sea* (1869-1870), *Around the world in eighty days* (1873), and *The mysterious island* (1875). He wrote about air, underwater, and space travel before they were invented.

Project 4

Yearbook

A school **yearbook** is a book to record, highlight, and commemorate the past year of the school.

Most American, Australian, and Canadian schools publish yearbooks. They can cover a wide variety of topics, such as academics, student life, sports, and other major school events. They can also include memorable events that occurred in that year. Generally, each student is pictured with their class.

Once the yearbooks are published, all the students sign each other's yearbooks with messages so they never forget their friends and the moments they had together.

1 Let's organize a yearbook!

a Divide the class into 5 groups. Give the instructions for each group.

Group 1: Make a list of all the school events of the past year and make notes about them.

Event	Date	What happened during the event?
....	....	....
....	....	....

Group 2: Make a list of the most memorable events that happened in Brazil and in the world in the past year and make notes about them.

Event	Date	Why was it memorable?
....	....	....
....	....	....

Group 3: Interview your classmates to find out memorable moments in their academic or personal life in the past year.

Name	Date	What happened?
....	....	....
....	....	....

Group 4: Interview your classmates to find out memorable moments they've had in the years they've studied at this school.

Name	Date	What happened?
....	....	....
....	....	....

Group 5: Interview your teachers and the school staff to find out what they will remember most about your class and your classmates.

Event	Date	What will they remember most?
....	....	....
....	....	....
....	....	....

b Find photographs that illustrate the information you collected in **a**.

c Rewrite your notes into paragraphs. Make it attractive and interesting! Revise your work.

d Edit your work: all the information and the photographs need to fit on two pages.

2 Let's finalize the yearbook!

Group 1: Make the yearbook cover. Write "Class of (year)" and create an attractive cover for your yearbook!

Group 2: Take a group photo and write an introduction to open the yearbook.

Group 3: Take photos of everyone in the class individually and organize the photos on three pages.

Group 4: Put the pages of yearbook together and organize an index and the credits. Follow this order:

Front cover	Back cover

Group photo and introduction (1)	Index (2)

Memorable events in Brazil and the world (3, 4)

School events of the past year (5, 6)

Memorable moments students have had in the years they've studied at this school (7, 8)

Memorable moments in students' academic or personal life (9, 10)

What teachers and the school staff will remember most about your class and your classmates (11, 12)

Individual photos page (13, 14, 15)	Credits (16)

Group 5: Proofread the yearbook and print it. Make one copy and ask your teacher or the principal to make copies for everyone else in the class.

3 Get a copy of your yearbook and pass it around so your classmates can sign it for you. Keep it. You will enjoy looking at it again in the future.

Looking Back at UNIT 5

Now I can...			Learn more about it:
read an obituary to learn about a person's life.			
talk about inspiration and motivation.			Read stories, comments, and advice by teenagers who talk about how to set and reach goals in *A taste-berry teen's guide to setting and achieving goals*, by Bettie B. Youngs and Jennifer Youngs.
read a text about sign language.			Learn to use *Libras* at <www.acessobrasil.org.br/libras>.
listen to a motivational speech.			Watch the movie *The pursuit of happiness* (2006) and learn the true story of Chris Gardner and what motivated him.
use the Present Perfect.			Study the information on page 144 in the *Grammar Reference* section.
use expressions to encourage and congratulate someone.			Watch the movie *Take the lead* (2006) and pay attention to the way the teacher in the movie encourages and congratulates his students.
use different intonations to express different feelings.			
analyze my attitudes to become a better student.			
write an obituary to reflect on and think about the future you want to have.			Watch the episode "Faith" from the TV series *The wonder years*.

Looking Back at UNIT 6

Now I can...			Learn more about it:
read newspaper headlines about the treatment of animals.			
talk about farm animals, meat, and produce.			Watch the movie *Animal farm* (1999), available at <www.imdb.com/title/tt0204824>.
practice the sounds / ɪ / and / i / to pronounce some words appropriately.			
read about Cesar Millan and learn more about being direct and consistent in your communication.			
read a text and infograph to learn about sustainable development.			Read more about how you can make the difference in an animal's life in *Kids making a difference for animals* (ASPCA Kids), by Nancy Furstinger and Shery L. Pipe.
listen to an opinion poll about people's opinions on humanizing pets.			
using *going to* to talk about the future.			Study the information on page 145 in the *Grammar Reference* section.
start, support, answer, and conclude arguments in a debate.			Read the book *Animal rights: noble cause or needless effort?* (USA Today's Debate: Voices and Perspectives).
write a petition to fight for a cause.			

Looking Back at UNIT 7

Now I can...			Learn more about it:
read quotations about future predictions.			Read other quotes at <www.quotationspage.com>.
use *will* and the correct pronunciation of its contraction to talk about the future.			Study the information on page 146 in the *Grammar Reference* section.
talk about the future.			
reflect on my mistakes to avoid repeating them in the future.			
discuss predictions about the future.			Watch movies that make predictions about the future, such as *Back to the future* (1985) and give your opinion about the predictions made.
listen to a song about how the singer feels about the future.			Watch the movie *Music and Lyrics* (2007) and learn the creative process of writing and composing a song.
read a text about Easter Island to reflect on how history can teach us to avoid repeating the same mistakes.			Watch *Rapa Nui* (1994) to learn more about Easter Island.
write predictions about the future to publish on a website.			

Looking Back at UNIT 8

Now I can...			Learn more about it:
read a manifesto to get general and specific information and make inferences from it.			Read other manifestos as the one available at <rightbrainterrain.com/Manifesto.htm>.
talk about future events in my life.			
listen to different accents to identify the speaker's origin.			Watch the movie *The world's fastest Indian* (2005) and notice how actor Anthony Hopkins, who is British, impersonates the Kiwi accent.
use conditionals to talk about what's necessary for something to happen.			Study the information on page 147 in the *Grammar Reference* section.
listen to a commencement address.			Listen to the commencement address done by the author of the Harry Potter series, JK Rowling, at <www.youtube.com/watch?feature=player_embedded&list=PLDE14B78238D691C0&v=nkREt4ZB-ck>.
use expressions to show nostalgia.			
control my anxiety and have a healthier life.			Read more about it in the book *The anxiety workout for teens: activities to help you deal with anxiety and worry*, by Lisa Schab.
read a text about the manifestos in the history of Brazilian art.			Look at the catalogue from one of the participants in the Brazilian Modern Art Week: Tarsila do Amaral, author of the *Abaporu*, available at <www.base7.com.br/tarsila>.
write a letter to my "future self" to set my goals for the future.			

Review Units 5 to 8

1 Complete the sentences with the Present Perfect of the verbs in parentheses.

a He .... a shower in a long time. (take)

b They .... in the woods. (walk)

c I .... my meal. (finish)

d She .... very busy. (be)

e It .... a lot of documents. (print)

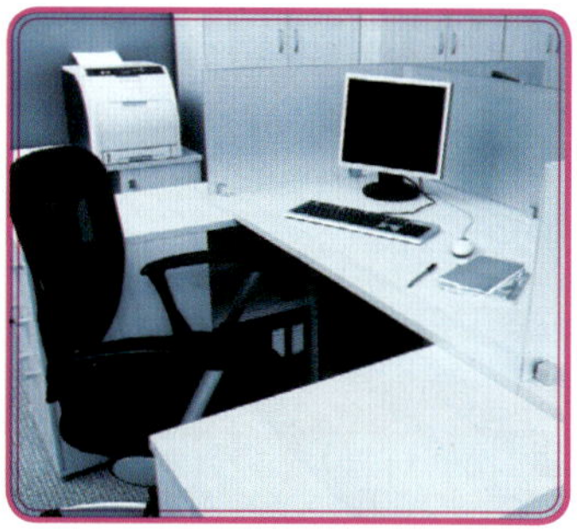

f .... he .... the office? (leave)

2 Complete the sentences with phrases from the box.

it will stop laying eggs for three days	the milk will taste like it	your back will hurt	it will eventually grow into a pig	it will become curious and come closer to you

a If you ride a horse for many hours, ...

b If you forget to feed the chicken, ...

c If you feed a cow with garlic, ...

d If you don't scare the lamb, ...

e Remember: if you have a piglet now, ...

3 **Look at the images and answer the questions using *going to*.**

a What is she going to do?

....

b Are they going to open a savings account?

....

c Are they going to move to a new house?

....

d What is she going to do?

....

e What are they going to do?

....

4 **Complete the dialog using *will* / *won't* and the verbs in parentheses.**

Wendy and Alan are shopping for groceries.

Wendy: I think I .... this new juice. (buy)

Alan: Hmm… Dad .... it. He always drinks the same juice. (like)

Wendy: Exactly. He .... to change some day, right? (have)

Alan: OK, but… .... to the supermarket to buy his favorite brand if he complains? (come back)

Wendy: No, ... He .... it if he doesn't have any other option. (drink)

Alan: Well, you know Dad… I think he .... to drink water if he doesn't like it. (prefer)

Grammar Reference

Unit 1

Simple Past

There are two kinds of verbs in the past: **regular** and **irregular**.

Regular verbs in the past end in **-ed**: enjoyed, learned, liked, listened, looked, loved, etc.

I enjoyed my free time.
She liked the movie.
They looked at the photos.

Irregular verbs in the past don't follow a rule (look at the list on page 150).

I spent some time in Europe.
He gave me a present for my birthday.
They took the bus to come here.

1 Write sentences about what these people did on their vacation.

visit a glacier • go surfing • ride a dune buggy • sing karaoke • see a soccer game • have a barbecue

a ....

b ....

c ....

d ....

e ....

f ....

2 What did you do on your vacation? Write 5 sentences.

....

....

....

....

Unit 2

Simple Past

Yes / no questions & short answers

- To form the **negative** in the Simple Past, add **didn't** after the subject and keep the verb in the infinitive without **to**.
  I didn't enjoy the last book of the series.
  She didn't like the movie.
  He didn't give me a present for my birthday.
  They didn't take the bus to come here.

- To form the **interrogative** in the Simple Past, add **did** before the subject and keep the verb in the infinitive without **to**. For **short answers**, use the auxiliaries **did** and **didn't**.
  Did you enjoy the weekend? Yes, I **did**. / No, I **didn't**.
  Did she take the dog for a walk? Yes, she **did**. / No, she **didn't**.
  Did they send the package? Yes, they **did**. / No, they **didn't**.

1 **Ask and answer about what these people did last weekend.**

a Did they ride their bikes in the park?
Yes, they did.

b ....?
No, ...

c ....?
No, ...

d ....?
Yes, ...

e ....?
No, ...

f ....?
Yes, ...

Unit 3

Modal verbs *must*, *might*, and *should*

Use ***must***, ***might***, or ***should*** and the main verb.

Must expresses obligation.
You ***must*** do your homework.

Might* / *might not expresses possibility.
The traffic is terrible. She ***might not*** come on time.

Must not* / *mustn't expresses prohibition.
You ***mustn't*** show disrespect for people's traditions.

Should* / *shouldn't expresses advice.
They ***should*** go to the beach more often.

***Might* want to** expresses polite advice.
You are tired. You ***might*** want to stay at home tonight.

1 Use the modal verbs to answer the questions or to complete the sentences about the photos.

a What's wrong with him?
(might) ....
(should) ....

b (must) ....
in the crosswalk.

c What's wrong with her?
(might) ....
(should) ....

d (mustn't) ....
without headphones on public transportation.

Unit 4

Passive voice

We often use the **passive voice** when it's not so important to mention **who** or **what** did the action.

The passive voice is formed by **object + verb *to be* + main verb in the past participle + complement**. The tense is determined by the **verb *to be***.

The room	was	cleaned	in the morning.
↓	↓	↓	↓
object	**verb *to be***	**main verb in the past participle**	**complement**
↑	↑	↑	↑
The evening TV news	is	recorded	in Miami.

The past participles of regular verbs end in **-ed**. For irregular verbs, use the third column of the list on page 150.

Now compare the same sentences in the **active voice**:

The students cleaned the room this morning.

Channel 6 records the evening TV news in Miami.

Notice that in the **active voice**, **who** or **what** did the action is an important information. Also notice that the order is **subject + main verb + object + complement**.

1 **Write A if the sentence is in the active voice and P if it is in the passive voice.**

a ◯ He adopted two kittens.

b ◯ The photographer took lots of photos for the new book.

c ◯ The robber was arrested.

d ◯ She was hired by another company.

e ◯ They leave their books at school.

f ◯ This computer is imported.

2 **Change the active voice sentences into passive voice sentences and vice versa.**
Tip: When you don't know the subject of the sentence, use "they".

a ....

b ....

c ....

d ....

e ....

f ....

Unit 5

Present Perfect

You can use abbreviations.
have = 've **has** = 's

Compare theses sentences:

Present Perfect	Simple Past
↓	↓
I've seen my best friend **this week.**	I **saw** my best friend **yesterday.**

We use the **Present Perfect** to talk about something that happened in a period of time that **is not** finished. We use the **Simple Past** to talk about something that happened in a period of time that **is** finished.

- The affirmative is formed by ***have / has* + the main verb in the past participle**.
  My friend **has seen** *The Lion King* five times!
  I **have been** to Manaus this year.
- The negative is formed by ***haven't / hasn't* + the main verb in the past participle**.
  My friend **hasn't seen** *The Lion King*.
  I **haven't been** to Manaus this year.
- The interrogative is formed by ***have / has* + subject + the main verb in the past participle**.
  Has she **seen** *The Lion King*?
  Have you **been** to Manaus this year?

1 Use the prompts to make questions and write true sentences about yourself and your friends and family.

a (I – watch TV today)
Have you watched TV today?
Yes, I have watched TV today. / No, I haven't watched TV today.

b (my father / mother – cook today)

....

....

c (my brother / sister – be to Manaus)

....

....

d (I – do the Portuguese homework this week)

....

....

e (my classmates and me – study together for the next tests)

....

....

f (my neighbor – buy a new bike this year)

....

....

Unit 6

Future with *going to*

Going to can be abbreviated to gonna in informal speech.

I'm going to watch a movie = I'm gonna watch a movie.

Use **going to** to talk about future plans.

subject / verb to be / going to / main verb	Example	Form
	I am going to take the bus to my grandparents' house in the countryside.	**Affirmative**
	She isn't going to come to our party because she needs to study.	**Negative**
	Are they going to send us the composition by email?	**Interrogative**

1 **Imagine you just won a scholarship to study English abroad. Choose one of these places to go and make plans. Complete the questions and write answers.**

New York, USA

Edinburgh, Scotland

Sydney, Australia

Cape town, South Africa

a When/travel?
When are you going to travel?
I'm going to travel in December.

b Where / study?

....

c What / do when you arrive there?

....

d Where / stay?

....

e Who / go with?

....

f What / take?

....

g How / travel around town?

....

h What / do when you have free time?

....

i When / come back?

....

2 **Compare your sentences with a classmate's. Write about his / her plans.**

....

....

3 **Write negative sentences about what you and your friend are not going to do there.**

....

....

....

Unit 7

Future with *will*

We use **will** to make predictions about the future.

subject will verb	Brazil will win the volleyball championship.	**Affirmative**
	The weather won't be good this weekend.	**Negative**
	Will he participate in the next elections?	**Interrogative**

1 Complete the questions and the answers appropriately.

a Will he go to school tomorrow? (to go)
I don't think so. I think he will stay at home. He's very sick. (to stay)

b .... at home tomorrow? (to stay)
I don't think so. He's feeling better, so I think .... to school. (to go)

c Where .... ? (to be)
I'm not sure. I think .... at the office. (to be)

d Who .... the petition to? (to send)
.... the petition to the principal, I guess. (to send)

e .... Brazilian food when you move to Japan? (to miss)
.... it much. I love Japanese food! (to miss; negative)

f When .... married? (to get)
They don't know yet. I think .... married only after they buy the apartment. (to get)

2 Write 6 predictions (3 in the affirmative, 3 in the negative) for next year.

a ....

b ....

c ....

d ....

e ....

f ....

Unit 8

Zero and first conditionals

Conditional sentences present **conditions** that are necessary for something to happen.

- The **zero conditional** is used to talk about scientific facts and general truths:
  If we leave an egg in boiling water for 10 minutes, it cooks.
  if-clause with Simple Present — clause with Simple Present
- The **zero conditional** can also be used to give instructions and advice.
  If you want to pass your exams, study hard!
  if-clause with Simple Present — clause with Imperative
- The **first conditional** is used to talk about possibilities for the future.
  If she comes home this weekend, we will have a big party for her.
  if-clause with Simple Present — clause with will

The order of the clauses is interchangeable:

If she comes home this weekend, we will have a big party for her.

↓

We will have a big party for her if she comes home this weekend.

1 Complete the sentences.

a If the weather is good this weekend, ...

b .... if I have money.

c If you visit Rio, ...

d If you stay in the sun for too long without sunscreen, ...

e If ...., don't cry! You will have another chance.

f We will travel if ....

A ⇄ B

UNIT 2 Page 31

2 Listen and repeat the conversations. 10

Agreeing with affirmative sentences	Agreeing with negative sentences
Me too.	Me neither.

A: I <u>watched</u> the movie Rango.

B: Me too. B: I didn't.

A: I <u>didn't watch</u> the movie Rango.

B: Me neither. B: I did.

3 Practice the dialog in pairs.

a Student B: Listen to Student A. Agree or disagree with him using short sentences.

b Student B: Now make true sentences about yourself using the prompts below. Does Student A agree or disagree with you?

1 I liked / didn't like emo music.

2 I wore / didn't wear rubber sandals.

3 I had / didn't have the happy family stickers.

Expressions to agree and disagree

- No way!
- I'm not so sure about that.
- Absolutely! But that's not the point!
- That's so true.
- Not necessarily.
- That's exactly what I was thinking!
- I guess so.

4 **Discuss the topic below. Use the expressions you learned to agree or disagree with your partner.**

It is OK to encourage people to consume cookies, considered as junk food, for a good cause.

Student A: Imagine you agree with the sentence. Use the arguments below and try to convince Student B.

- Buying the cookies doesn't mean you're going to eat them all.
- You don't have to keep the boxes of cookies. You can buy them and leave them as a donation to the Girl Scouts.
- The Girl Scout cookies have "zero trans fat per serving" and no preservatives, so they are not as bad as many other foods you normally consume.

Irregular verbs

Infinitive	Past	Participle	Tradução
be	was, were	been	ser, estar
become	became	become	tornar-se
begin	began	begun	começar
break	broke	broken	quebrar, interromper
bring	brought	brought	trazer
build	built	built	construir
buy	bought	bought	comprar
catch	caught	caught	agarrar, pegar (doença)
choose	chose	chosen	escolher
come	came	come	vir, chegar, aproximar-se, acontecer
cost	cost	cost	custar
cut	cut	cut	cortar
deal	dealt	dealt	negociar, distribuir
do	did	done	fazer, executar
draw	drew	drawn	desenhar, puxar, arrastar
dream	dreamt / dreamed	dreamt / dreamed	sonhar
drink	drank	drunk	beber, embriagar-se
drive	drove	driven	dirigir
eat	ate	eaten	comer
fall	fell	fallen	cair
feed	fed	fed	alimentar, suprir
feel	felt	felt	sentir
find	found	found	encontrar
fly	flew	flown	voar
forget	forgot	forgotten	esquecer (se)
get	got	got / gotten	conseguir, ganhar
give	gave	given	dar, conceder
go	went	gone	ir
grow	grew	grown	crescer, cultivar
have	had	had	ter, possuir
hear	heard	heard	ouvir
hold	held	held	segurar, manter, conter
hurt	hurt	hurt	machucar
keep	kept	kept	guardar, manter, permanecer, ficar
know	knew	known	saber, conhecer
learn	learnt	learnt	aprender
leave	left	left	deixar, partir
lend	lent	lent	emprestar
let	let	let	deixar, alugar
lie	lay	lain	deitar

Infinitive	Past	Participle	Tradução
lose	lost	lost	perder
make	made	made	fazer, produzir, fabricar
mean	meant	meant	significar, ter a intenção de
meet	met	met	encontrar-se com
pay	paid	paid	pagar
put	put	put	pôr
read	read	read	ler
ride	rode	ridden	viajar, cavalgar
ring	rang	rung	soa , tocar a campainha
rise	rose	risen	nascer, surgir, erguer-se
run	ran	run	correr, administrar
say	said	said	dizer
see	saw	seen	ver
sell	sold	sold	vender
send	sent	sent	enviar
set	set	set	colocar, fixar, arrumar
show	showed	shown / showed	mostrar
sing	sang	sung	cantar
sit	sat	sat	sentar
sleep	slept	slept	dormir
smell	smelt	smelt	cheirar
speak	spoke	spoken	falar
spend	spent	spent	gastar
spread	spread	spread	difundir, divulgar, espalhar
stand	stood	stood	ficar de pé, aguentar
steal	stole	stolen	roubar
strike	struck	struck	fazer greve, bater
swear	swore	sworn	jurar, blasfemar
swim	swam	swum	nadar
swing	swung	swung	balançar
take	took	taken	tomar, pegar
teach	taught	taught	ensinar
tell	told	told	contar, dizer
think	thought	thought	pensar, achar
throw	threw	thrown	arremessar
understand	understood	understood	entender, compreender
wake	woke	woke	acordar
wear	wore	worn	vestir, usar
wed	wed	wed	desposar
wet	wet	wet	umedecer
win	won	won	ganhar, vencer
write	wrote	written	escrever

Minidictionary

English-Portuguese

More than 900 entries!

WITH STAR RATING

adj. = adjective
adv. = adverb
conj. = conjunction
deter. = determiner
interj. = interjection
mod. v. = modal verb
n. = noun
numb. = number
prep. = preposition
pron. = pronoun
v. = verb

All red words have a "star rating":

★★★ The most common and basic English words.

★★ Very common words

★ Fairly common words

A

abandoned /ə'bændənd/ adj. abandonado *This is a home for abandoned children.*

ability /ə'bɪləti/ n. ★★★ habilidade *He has the ability to roll his tongue.*

about /ə'baʊt/ adv. prep. ★★★ sobre *I like to talk about films.*

above /ə'bʌv/ adv. ★★★ acima *The picture is above the sofa.*

absolutely /'æbsəlutli/ adv. ★★★ absolutamente *The food was absolutely fantastic.*

absorbing /əb'sɔrbɪŋ/ adj. absorvente, envolvente *I am reading a really absorbing book.*

abundant /ə'bʌndənt/ adj. abundante *The country has an abundant supply of grains.*

accent /'æk,sent/ n. ★★ sotaque *Tom hasn't lost his strong Irish accent.*

accomplish /ə'kʌmplɪʃ/ v. ★★ cumprir uma tarefa *We didn't accomplish much at work this week.*

across /ə'krɔs/ adv. ★★★ do outro lado de *There is a hostel across the street.*

achieve /ə'tʃiv/ v. ★★★ alcançar, conseguir *His paintings did not achieve the popularity of his books.*

activist /'æktɪvɪst/ n. ★ ativista *My uncle and my aunt are environmental activists.*

actually /'æktʃuəli/ adv. ★★★ na verdade *He is not my brother; he is actually my cousin.*

address /ə'dres/ n. ★★★ endereço *I wrote his address in this notebook.*

adopt /ə'dɑpt/ v. ★★★ adotar *The couple are hoping to adopt a baby girl.*

advertise /'ædvər,taɪz/ v. ★★ anunciar *They advertise all kinds of products on TV.* **advertised** anunciado

affect /ə'fekt/ v. ★★★ afetar *The disease affects many different organs of the body.*

after /'æftər/ adv. ★★★ depois *I brush my teeth after eating.*

against /ə'genst/ prep. ★★★ contra *I'm against all forms of censorship.*

age /eɪdʒ/ n. ★★ idade, era *What's his age? He's eleven.*

ageism /'eɪ,dʒɪzəm/ n. discriminação contra idade *We do not accept ageism here.*

agree /ə'gri/ v. ★★★ concordar *We all agree that we should celebrate this event.*

ahead /ə'hed/ adv. à frente *There's a supermarket just a few kilometers ahead.*

allow /ə'loʊn/ v. ★★★ permitir *You are not allowed to run here.*

almost /'ɔlmoʊst/ adv. ★★★ quase *It's almost 9 pm Let's go to bed.*

alone /ə'laʊ/ adj. adv. ★★★ sozinho *Ady never stays alone at home.*

already /ɔl'redi/ adv. ★★★ já *It's 7 pm and he is already sleeping.*

ambassador /æm'bæsədər/ n. ★★ embaixador *Paul is the Egyptian ambassador to Belize.*

amount /ə'maʊnt/ n. ★★★ quantidade (de algo) *A computer can store a vast amount of information.*

amount to phrasal verb somar à *The results of the research don't really amount to much.*

analysis /ə'næləsɪs/ n. ★★★ análise *In the final analysis, it is up to the students to decide.*

angel /'eɪndʒəl/ n. ★★ anjo *Be an angel and get me a cup of coffee.*

answer /'ænsər/ n. v. ★★ resposta, responder *The correct answer is B.*

anticipate /æn'tɪsɪ,peɪt/ v. ★★ antecipar *We anticipate that the river level will rise very slowly.*

anywhere /'eni,wer/ adv. ★★★ em qualquer lugar *He never travels anywhere without his camera.*

appear /ə'pɪr/ v. ★★★ parecer, aparecer *This exercise is not as difficult as it appears to be.*

appearance /ə'pɪrəns/ n. ★★★ aparência *The twins are almost identical in appearance.*

application /,æplɪ'keɪʃ(ə)n/ n. ★★★ inscrição *The university welcomes applications from older students.*

apply /ə'plaɪ/ v. ★★★ inscrever-se *Students can apply for money to help with their living costs.*

appreciate /ə'priʃi,eɪt/ v. ★★ apreciar *She feels that her family doesn't really appreciate her.*

appropriate /ə'proʊpriət/ adj. ★★★ apropriado; correto *Fill in the blank with the appropriate word.*

April /'eɪprəl/ n. ★★★ abril *My birthday is in April.*

arcade /ɑr'keɪd/ n. ★★ arcada *There are beautiful flowers under the arcades.*

argument /'ɑrgjəmənt/ n. ★★★ discussão *We had an argument about our chores at home.*

arm /ɑrm/ n. ★★★ braço *I put my arm around his shoulders.*

arrive /ə'raɪv/ v. ★★★ chegar *The taxi will arrive at 8 o'clock.*

as well phrase também *I'd like a cup of coffee, and a glass of water as well.*

assume /ə'sum/ v. ★★★ presumir *I think we can assume that he is out of town.*

attendance /ə'tendəns/ n. ★★ frequência, público *Church attendance dropped sharply in the 1970s.*

attention /ə'tenʃ(ə)n/ n. ★★★ atenção *May I please have your attention?*

attractive /ə'træktɪv/ adj. ★★★ atraente *We saw a less attractive side of his personality that day.*

audience /'ɔdiəns/ n. ★★★ público, audiência *The series has attracted an audience of more than 10 million.*

autumn /'ɔtəm/ n. ★ outono *We haven't heard from him since last autumn.*

aversion /ə'vɜrʒ(ə)n/ n. aversão *Some people have an aversion to reptiles.*

avocado /,ævə'kɑdoʊ/ n. abacate *Children love avocado cream.*

avoid /ə'vɔɪd/ v. ★★★ evitar *Vitor avoids eating meat.*

award /ə'wɔrd/ n. ★★★ prêmio *She won the Player of the Year award.*

awesome /'ɔsəm/ adj. incrível *2008 was an awesome year!*

B

bad /bæd/ adj. ★★★ mau *The teacher is bad-humored today.*

badly /'bædli/ adv. ★★★ mal *She feels she has been badly treated.*

bake /beɪk/ v. ★ assar *Bake the fish for about ten minutes.*

baking soda /'beɪkɪŋ ,soʊdə/ n. bicarbonato *Do not forget to add baking soda to the bread dough.*

bang (usually used in the plural) /'bæŋz/ n. franja *Her bangs are getting really long; I can't see her eyes.*

be /bi/ v. ★★★ ser *The orchestra will be conducted by David Norton.*

be able to /bi 'eɪb(ə)l tə/ phrase ser apto a *Mirian is able to take care of herself.*

be born phrasal verb nascer *He was born in November, 1964.*

beach /bitʃ/ n. ★★★ praia *Going to the beach is my favorite vacation activity.*

beauty /'bjuti/ n. ★★★ beleza *She was a great beauty in her time.*

because /bɪ'kɔz/ conj. ★★★ porque *The floor is wet because it rained.*

become /bɪ'kʌm/ v. ★★★ transformar-se, vir a ser *Christine decided to become a writer.*

beef /bif/ n. ★★ bife *Vegetarians do not eat beef.*

before /bɪ'fɔr/ adv. ★★★ antes *Brush your teeth before going to bed.*

begin /bɪ'gɪn/ v. ★★★ começar *The ceremony is due to begin at noon.*

beginning /bɪ'gɪnɪŋ/ n. ★★★ começo *We missed the beginning of the film.*

behavior /bɪ'heɪvjər/ n. ★★★ comportamento *Anna was sick of her brother's annoying behavior.*

behind /bɪ'haɪnd/ adv. prep. ★★★ atrás *The car is behind the tree.*

belief /bɪ'lif/ n. ★★★ crença *There is a growing belief that she will resign.*

believe /b□□liv/ v. ★★★ acreditar *Astronomers knew the Earth was round, but few people believed them.*

belong /bɪ'lɔŋ/ v. ★★★ pertencer *When you're done, put the books back where they belong.*

below /bɪ'ləʊ/ adv. ★★★ abaixo *The basement is below the house.*

besides /bɪ'saɪdz/ adv. prep. ★★ além disso *A lot of them are studying other languages besides Italian.*

best /best/ adj. ★★★ melhor *Rory and Jade are best friends.*

better /'betər/ adj. ★★★ melhor *Fernando is better in math than Cláudio.*

between /bɪ'twin/ adv. ★★★ entre *The church is between the bank and the supermarket.*

bike /baɪk/ n. ★★ bicicleta *Their favorite sport is to ride a bike.*

bill /bɪl/ n. ★★★ conta *I will pay the telephone bill this afternoon.*

bin /bɪn/ n. ★ cesto *We have bins for recycled trash in our school.*

biodegradable /ˌbaɪoʊdɪ'greɪdəb(ə)l/ adj. biodegradável *We use biodegradable detergent at home.*

bionic /baɪ'ɑnɪk/ adj. biônico *He has a bionic leg.*

birthday /'bɜrθˌdeɪ/ n. ★★ aniversário *Today is her birthday party.*

blank /blæŋk/ n. lacuna *Please put either a check or an X in the blanks.*

body /'bɑdi/ n. ★★★ corpo *My body hurts because I exercised too much.*

boil /bɔɪl/ v. ★ ferver *Water boils at 100 °C.*

book /bʊk/ n. ★★★ livro *This atlas is my least favorite book.*

boring /'bɔrɪŋ/ adj. ★★ chato *It gets boring just being at home all day.*

both /boʊθ/ det. pron. ★★★ ambos *Both my parents are doctors.*

box /bɑks/ n. ★★★ caixa *Put the toys in the box.*

bra /brɑ/ n. ★ sutiã *This bra is too small for me.*

brain /breɪn/ n. ★★★ cérebro *The brain is the most important part of the human body.*

bread /bred/ n. ★★★ pão *Ana loves bread with butter.*

break /breɪk/ v. ★★★ quebrar *Break the spaghetti in half and put it into the boiling water.*

bridge /brɪdʒ/ n. ★★★ ponte *We walked across a wooden bridge.*

bring /brɪŋ/ v. ★★★ trazer *You cannot bring pets to school.*

brotherhood /'brʌðərˌhʊd/ n. irmandade *He taught us freedom, tolerance, and brotherhood.*

budget /'bʌdʒət/ n. ★★★ orçamento *All schools are expected to manage their own budgets.*

build /bɪld/ v. ★★★ construir *They are building a shopping mall near my house.*

bunch /bʌntʃ/ n. ★★ grupo *The volunteers are a very mixed bunch of people.*

burn /bɜrn/ v. ★★★ queimar *Have you burned the toast again?*

business /'bɪznəs/ n. ★★★ negócio *They have a restaurant as their business.*

buy /baɪ/ v. ★★★ comprar *I buy food for the week.*

C

cafeteria /ˌkæfə'tɪriə/ n. cantina *The students met in the cafeteria for lunch.*

cage /keɪdʒ/ n. ★ gaiola *The tiger is kept in a cage in the zoo.*

calf /kæf/ n. bezerro *The cow had a calf last night.*

call /kɔːl/ v. ★★★ chamar, ligar *They call Rebecca Beckie.*

calligraphy /kə'lɪgrəfi/ n. caligrafia *Steve Jobs studied calligraphy.*

camp /kæmp/ v. ★ acampar *They camp every summer.*

campaign /kæm'peɪn/ n. ★★★ campanha *It is a campaign againt prejudice.*

cannibal /'kænɪb(ə)l/ n. canibal, quem se alimenta de carne humana *This is a cannibal tribe.*

cannot /'kæˌnɑt/ mod. v. ★★★ não poder *You cannot escape the law.*

canoe /kə'nu/ n. ★ canoa *They crossed the river using that canoe.*

cap /kæp/ n. ★★ boné *Wear a cap when inside the caverns.*

capable /'keɪpəb(ə)l/ adj. ★★★ capaz *The staff all seem very capable.*

careful /'kerf(ə)l/ adj. ★★★ cuidadoso *Please be very careful with those plates!*
carefully cuidadosamente

car /kɑr/ n. ★★★ carro *My aunt's car is red.*

carry /'keri/ v. ★★★ carregar *Can you carry these bags?*

catch /kætʃ/ v. ★★★ pegar *We catch the bus at that stop over there.*

cave /keɪv/ n. ★★ caverna *In Bonito, there is a beautiful lake inside a cave.*

celebrate /'seləˌbreɪt/ v. ★★★ celebrar *Let's have a party to celebrate your birthday.*

certain /'sɜrt(ə)n/ adj. certeza, certo *I am certain he is in school today.*

certainty /'sɜrt(ə)nti/ n. ★★ certeza *Victory looked like a certainty, but then we lost three games back to back.*

change /tʃeɪndʒ/ v. n. ★★★ trocar, troco *Change those clothes, it is cold!*

challenge /'tʃæləndʒ/ n. ★★★ desafio *Playing cards with my grandmother is a real challenge: she is so good!*

chat /tʃæt/ n. v. ★★ bate-papo; bater papo *I had an interesting chat with his sister.*

check /tʃek/ v. ★★★ checar, marcar *Check the correct answers.*

chest /tʃest/ n. ★★★ peito *Have you had any chest pains?*

chick /tʃɪk/ n. pintinho de galinha *At my grandpa's house I always play with the little chicks.*

chicken /'tʃɪkən/ n. ★★ frango *Chicken is a traditional dish in India.*

chickpea /'tʃɪkˌpi/ n. grão de bico *Hommus is made from chickpeas.*

children /'tʃɪldrən/ plural of child crianças *Children must not work.*

choice /tʃɔɪs/ n. ★★★ escolha *Our aim is to provide greater choice for consumers.*

choose /tʃuz/ v. ★★★ escolher *I always choose pineapple ice cream.*

chorus /'kɔrəs/ n. ★ refrão *He encouraged the audience to join in the chorus.*

circus /'sɜrkəs/ n. circo *The kids want us to take them to the circus again.*

citizen /'sɪtɪz(ə)n/ n. ★★★ cidadão *She married an American and became a U.S. citizen.*

city /'sɪti/ n. ★★★ cidade *São Paulo is the biggest Brazilian city.*

clean /klin/ v. adj. ★★★ limpar, limpo *Clean your bedroom, please.*

close /kloʊz/ v. n. ★★★ fechar; próximo *It's windy; close the window, please.*

clothes /kloʊðz/ n. ★★★ roupas *Alice's clothes are new.*

coach /koʊtʃ/ n. ★★ treinador *Our coach is also our PE teacher.*

coconut /'koʊkəˌnʌt/ n. coco *They love drinking coconut water.*

coexist /ˌkoʊɪg'zɪst/ v. coexistir *These communities have peacefully coexisted for centuries.*

coffee /'kɑfi/ n. ★★★ café *Helen drinks coffee with milk every morning.*

coherent /koʊ'hɪrənt/ adj. ★ coerente *This text is not coherent.*

collapse /kə'læps/ n. v. ★★ colapso; colapsar *The economy is in a state of collapse.*

collector /kə'lektər/ n. ★★ colecionador *My brother is a stamp collector.*

college /'kalɪdʒ/ n. ★★★ faculdade *Paul's going to college in September.*

come /kʌm/ v. ★★★ vir *The stickers come with the album.*

comma /'kamə/ n. ★ vírgula *A comma is a kind of punctuation.*

commit /kə'mɪt/ v. ★★★ cometer; comprometer *Reports suggest that the singer committed suicide.*

comparable /'kamp(ə)rəb(ə)l/ adj. ★★ comparável *The salary is comparable to that of a junior doctor.*

complain /kəm'pleɪn/ v. ★★★ reclamar *Those tourists complain all the time.*

condemned /kən'demd/ adj. condenado *He was condemned for the crime.*

condition /kən'dɪʃ(ə)n/ n. ★★★ estado físico (médico) *She's in excellent physical condition.*

confined /kən'faɪnd/ adj. confinado *Reality show participants have to stay confined for a long time.*

confinement /kən'faɪnmənt/ n. confinamento *She started writing poetry during her long confinement in prison.*

confusing /kən'fjuzɪŋ/ adj. ★ confuso *Some of the questions he asked were very confusing.*

congratulate /kən'grætʃə,leɪt/ v. ★ parabenizar *I congratulated him on his recent promotion.*

congratulation /kən,grætʃə'leɪʃ(ə)n/ n. ★ parabéns *That's great news – give her my congratulations.*

connect /kə'nekt/ v. ★★★ conectar, ligar *She carefully connected the two wires.*

conquer /'kaŋkər/ v. ★ conquistar *His gentle nature had conquered their hearts.*

consequently /'kansəkwəntli/ adv. ★★ consequentemente *They've increased the number of staff, and consequently, the service is better.*

consist /kən'sɪst/ v. ★★★ consistir *True strength does not consist in mere muscle.*

constantly /'kanstəntli/ adv. ★★ constantemente *We are constantly reminded of his success.*

contagious /kən'teɪdʒəs/ adj. contagioso *That disease is not contagious.*

contribution /,kantrɪ'bjuʃ(ə)n/ n. ★★★ contribuição *This cake is my contribution to the meal.*

cook /kʊk/ v. ★★★ cozinhar *Marnie will cook something delicious tonight.*

cookie /'kʊki/ n. ★★ biscoito *We love having cookies with milk.*

cool down phrasal verb resfriar; relaxar *Wait for the dish to cool down before opening the oven.*

could /kʊd/ mod. v ★★★ poderia *Could you give me the keys?*

countryside /'kʌntri,saɪd/ n. ★ interior, zona rural *They have a beautiful house in the countryside.*

cow /kaʊ/ n. ★★ vaca *This cow produces a lot of milk.*

cracker /'krækər/ n. bolacha (salgada) *They have tea and crackers as a snack.*

creative /kri'eɪtɪv/ adj. ★ criativo *Creative people tend to be happier.*

crispy /'krɪspi/ adj. crocante *This chicken nugget is really crispy.*

critical /'krɪtɪk(ə)l/ adj. ★★★ crítico *This is a critical moment for our team.*

crossword /'krɔs,wɜrd/ n. ★ palavras cruzadas *Crosswords are my favorite pastime.*

crowded /'kraʊdəd/ adj. ★ lotado *The concert is so crowded!*

cruelty /'kruəlti/ n. ★ crueldade *We do not accept cruelty against children and animals.*

crumbly /'krʌmbli/ adj. esfarelento *Hannah finds it difficult to eat crumbly bread.*

cultivated /'kʌltɪ,veɪtəd/ adj. cultivado *These fruits are organically cultivated.*

cut down (on) phrasal verb reduzir *We need to cut down on our energy consumption.*

D

daily /'deɪli/ adj. ★★★ diário *We exercise daily.*

damage /'dæmɪdʒ/ v. n. ★★★ danificar; dano *The rain caused a lot of damage in the town.*

dance /dæns/ n. v. ★★★ dança; dançar *Sheila and Sonja know how to dance really well.* **dancer** dançarino

date /deɪt/ n. ★★★ encontro, data *Tomorrow is the final date for the contest applications.*

day /deɪ/ n. ★★★ dia *I have a shower every day.*

day-to-day adj. (only before noun) ★ diário *Walking the dog is part of her day-to-day activities.*

dead /ded/ adj. ★★★ morto *There were two injured and one dead victim in the accident.*

deal /dil/ v. ★★★ lidar *You should deal with that situation with a little more calm.*

dear /dɪr/ adj. ★★★ querido; querida *Dear John, I miss you.*

deaf /def/ adj. ★★ surdo *She's been totally deaf since birth.*

deafness n. surdez *Scientists are trying to find a cure for deafness.*

declaration /,deklə'reɪʃ(ə)n/ n.. ★★ declaração *She was not convinced by his declaration of love.*

declare /dɪ'kler/ v. ★★★ declarar *"I'm leaving tomorrow," James suddenly declared.*

decline /dɪ'klaɪn/ v. ★★★ declinar, recusar *The number of people buying their own homes has declined.*

dedicated /'dedɪ,keɪtəd/ adj. ★ dedicado *He was very hard-working and dedicated to his research.*

definitely /'defənɪtli/ adv. ★★ definitivamente *That's definitely not the man I saw running away.*

deliver /dɪ'lɪvər/ v. ★★★ entregar *The package was delivered this morning.*

demand /dɪ'mænd/ v. ★★★ pedir, demandar *I demand a lot of others but more of myself.*

deny /dɪ'naɪ/ v. ★★★ negar *All three athletes vehemently deny talking the drug.*

describe /dɪ'skraɪb/ v. ★★★ descrever *Look at the picture and describe what you see.* **description** descrição

dessert /dɪ'zɜrt/ n. ★★ sobremesa *Would you like mousse or fruit for dessert?*

detail /dɪ'teɪl/ n. ★ detalhe *Pay attention to the details of the image.*

devour /dɪ'vaʊr/ v. devorar *The tsunami devoured the beaches.*

dialog /'daɪəlɒg/ n. ★★ diálogo *Listen to the dialog between Bruno and Jeff.*

die /daɪ/ v. ★★★ morrer *They were ready to die for their country.*

diet /'daɪət/ n. dieta *You should include more vegetables in your diet.*

differ /'dɪfər/ v. diferir *English differs from Spanish in that it is not pronounced as it is written.*

dinner /'dɪnər/ n. ★★★ jantar *We have dinner at 8:00 pm.*

disabled /dɪ'seɪb(ə)ld/ adj. ★★ deficiente *This parking lot is for disabled drivers.*

disagree /,dɪsə'gri/ v. ★★ discordar *We disagree on almost everything.*

disappear /,dɪsə'pɪr/ v. ★★★ desaparecer *The symptoms should disappear within a few days.*

disappointed /,dɪsə'pɔɪntəd/ adj. ★ desapontado *She was disappointed that he never replied to her letter.*

discover /dɪ'skʌvər/ v. ★★★ descobrir *He became very friendly when he discovered that she was my sister.*

discrimination /dɪ,skrɪmɪ'neɪʃ(ə)n/ n. ★★ discriminação *Discrimination on the grounds of sex or race is unlawful.*

dish /dɪʃ/ n. ★★ prato *Her favorite dish is fried chicken.*

display /dɪ'spleɪ/ v. dispor *Display the cards on the table.*

disposal /dɪ'spoʊz(ə)l/ n. ★★ descarte *The disposal of nuclear waste at sea should be banned.*

dispose /dɪ'spoʊz/ v. ★★ descartar *Dispose of your ice-cream wrapper in the trash can.*

disappointing /ˌdɪsə'pɔɪntɪŋ/ adj. ★ frustrante *The result of the game was disappinting.*

distracted /dɪ'stræktəd/ adj. distraído *All that summer Rosie seemed distant and distracted.*

disturb /dɪ'stɜrb/ v. ★★ atrapalhar *I didn't want to disturb you in the middle of a meeting.*

do /du/ v. ★★★ fazer *Do your homework before watching TV.*

donate /'doʊˌneɪt/ v. ★ **doar** *I will donate the toys I do not like anymore.* **donation** doação

door /dɔr/ n. ★★★ porta *Come in and close the door.*

dough /doʊ/ n. massa (de bolo, de pão) *Mix the flour, the milk, the eggs, and the sugar to form a dough.*

draft /dræft/ n. ★★ rascunho *This is just a draft; I'll give you the composition tomorrow.*

dramatic /drə'mætɪk/ adj. ★★★ dramático *Don't be so dramatic!*

dramatically /drə'mætɪkli/ adv. dramaticamente *The weather changed dramatically yesterday.*

dream /drim/ v. n. ★★ sonhar; sonho *I never remember my dreams.*

dress /dres/ v. n. ★★★ vestir; vestido **doll dress** vestido de boneca *Lacey's dress is blue.*

drink /drɪŋk/ v. n. ★★★ beber; bebida *You should drink a lot of water every day.*

drop into phrasal verb cair, jogar-se *Teresa dropped into the chair, exhausted.*

drop out phrasal verb abandonar *Too many students drop out of college after only one year.*

dry /draɪ/ adj. ★★★ seco *The chicken was overcooked and dry.*

duck /dʌk/ n. ★★ pato *Duck is commonly eaten in Pará.*

duckling /'dʌklɪŋ/ n. patinho *Ducklings are really cute small birds.*

due to prep. ★★★ por causa de *His illness is due to his poor diet.*

dull /dʌl/ adj. ★★ chato, sem graça *This is a dull game.*

during /'djʊərɪŋ/ prep. ★★★ durante *The baby generally sleeps during the night.*

E

earn /ɜrn/ v. ★★★ ganhar *You have to earn your employees' respect.*

Earth /ɜrθ/ n. ★★★ Terra *The Moon goes around the Earth.*

Easter /'istər/ n. ★ Páscoa *The kids get two weeks off school at Easter.*

eat /it/ v. ★★★ comer *It's dinner time: let's eat!*

effort /'efərt/ n. ★★★ esforço *I've made an effort to drink less tea and coffee.*

egg /eg/ n. ★★★ ovo *Pamela loves fried eggs.*

elephant /'eləfənt/ n. ★ elefante *There are no elephants in this zoo.*

emphasis /'emfəsɪs/ n. ★★★ ênfase *The main emphasis should be on quality rather than quantity.*

enable /ɪn'eɪb(ə)l/ v. ★★★ habilitar *This will enable users to conduct live video conversations.*

encourage /ɪn'kʌrɪdʒ/ v. ★★★ encorajar *We encourage student participation in our classes.*

encouragement /ɪn'kʌrɪdʒmənt/ n. ★★ encorajamento *We needed you there to offer words of encouragement.*

end /end/ n. ★★★ fim *The end of the book is very sad.*

endangered /ɪn'deɪndʒərd/ adj. em extinção *There are more then 50 endangered species protected in this zoo.*

endow /ɪn'daʊ/ v. doar *He endows part of his earnings to the city hospital.*

enemy /'enəmi/ n. ★★★ inimigo *It's easy to make enemies in a job like this.*

energetic /ˌenər'dʒetɪk/ adj. ★ energético *He is a smart and energetic boy.*

energy /'enərdʒi/ n. ★★★ energia *Turn off the lights to save energy.*

enjoy /ɪn'dʒɔɪ/ v. ★★★ curtir, desfrutar *Nina enjoys playing with dogs.*

enough /ɪ'nʌf/ adv. ★★★ o suficiente *Do not put sugar in the juice. It's sweet enough.*

entitle /ɪn'taɪt(ə)l/ v. ★★ intitular *Her first novel was entitled More Innocent Times.*

environmental /ɪnˌvaɪrən'ment(ə)l/ adj. ★★★ ambiental *Both candidates discussed environmental issues.*

every /'evri/ det. ★★★ todo *Josh visits his grandparents every week.*

everything /'evriˌθɪŋ/ pron. ★★★ tudo *I will do everything for this team.*

excerpt /'ekˌsɜrpt/ n. excerto *Read the excerpt and answer these questions.*

excited /ɪk'saɪtəd/ adj. ★★ agitado, empolgado *Flávio and Fred are really excited about the trip.*

exciting /ɪk'saɪtɪŋ/ adj. ★★ estimulante *I read an exciting story of adventure.*

exemplify /ɪg'zemplɪˌfaɪ/ v. exemplificar *I will exemplify my point with a true story about something that happened to me.*

expensive /ɪk'spensɪv/ adj. ★★★ caro *This skirt is too expensive. I will buy the other one.*

explain /ɪk'spleɪn/ v. ★★★ explicar *I will try to explain how this machine works.*

express /ɪk'spres/ v. ★★★ expressar *His teachers expressed concern about his progress at school.*

extinct /ɪk'stɪŋkt/ adj. ★ extinto *The Tasmanian tiger was declared extinct in 1936.*

F

facility /fə'sɪləti/ n. ★★★ recursos *The hotel has excellent recreational facilities.*

fact /fækt/ n. ★★★ fato *Read the story and summarize the facts.*

factory /'fækt(ə)ri/ n. ★★★ fábrica *She works in a factory.*

fad /fæd/ n. modinha, moda passageira *Virtual pets were a fad among teens in the 1990s.*

fair /feə(r)/ adj. ★★★ feira *Bienal is a Brazilian book fair.*

fall /fɔl/ v. ★★★ cair *It's not unusual for small children to fall out of bed.*

family /'fæm(ə)li/ n. ★★★ família *There are more than 60 members in my family.*

FAQ /ˌef eɪ 'kju/ n. perguntas frequentes *Check your doubts on the FAQ page.*

farm /fɑrm/ n. ★★★ fazenda *My grandparents live in a farm with many animals.*

farmer /'fɑrmər/ n. ★★★ fazendeiro *The farmer lives on the farm with his family.*

fat-free adj. sem gordura *This is a fat-free yogurt.*

February /'februˌeri/ n. ★★★ fevereiro *I'm starting my new job in February.*

feed /fid/ v. ★★★ alimentar *Cesar and Andre feed their cats twice a day.*

feel /fil/ v. ★★★ sentir *I feel sick. I want to stay home.* **feeling** sentimento

feeling /'filɪŋ/ n. ★★★ sentimento *Love is a good feeling.*

foot /fʊt/ n. ★★★ pé *My foot hurts when I walk too much.* **feet** pés

few /fju/ det. pron. ★★★ poucos *Students, you have just a few minutes to hand in your compositions.*

field /fild/ n. ★★★ campo *There were horses grazing in the next field.*

filling /'fɪlɪŋ/ n. recheio *My grandma made a pie with cherry filling.*

finally /ˈfaɪn(ə)li/ adv. ★★★ finalmente *We finally arrived home at midnight.*

find /faɪnd/ v. ★★★ encontrar **find out** descobrir *I want to find out what time the film starts.*

finish /ˈfɪnɪʃ/ v. ★★★ terminar *I finish the homework before watching TV.*

firefighter /ˈfaɪrˌfaɪtər/ n. bombeiro *Some of these firefighters are paramedics too.*

firework /ˈfaɪrˌwɜrk/ n. ★ fogos de artifício *There was a great fireworks show at the party.*

first /fɜrst/ numb. ★★★ primeiro *The first day of the week is Sunday.*

fish /fɪʃ/ n. v. ★★★ peixe; pescar *We will have fish for dinner tonight.*

fix /fɪks/ v. ★★★ consertar *Jessica fixed my watch.*

flesh /fleʃ/ n. ★★ carne *I felt the soft flesh of his cheek.*

flour /flaʊr/ n. ★ farinha *Add two tablespoons of flour.*

fluent /ˈfluənt/ adj. ★ fluente *Steve speaks fluent Japanese.*

fluid /ˈfluɪd/ n. ★ fluído, líquido *Drink lots of fluids during exercise.*

fly /flaɪ/ v. ★★★ voar *Sometimes it's cheaper to fly.*

foal /foʊl/ n. potro *Foals drink many liters of milk in their first weeks of life.*

follow /ˈfɑloʊ/ v. ★★★ seguir *Follow good examples.*

food /fud/ n. ★★★ comida *Food is good for your body.*

foolish /ˈfulɪʃ/ adj. ★ bobo *I felt so foolish when I realized what I had done.*

football /ˈfʊtˌbɔl/ n. ★★★ futebol (americano) *My favorite sports are football and hockey.*

foreign /ˈfɔrən/ adj. ★★★ estrangeiro *Do you speak any foreign languages?*

foreigner /ˈfɔrənər/ n. ★★ estrangeiro *Mark is a foreigner.*

forest /ˈfɔrəst/ n. ★★★ floresta *Acid rain is already destroying large areas of forest.*

forget /fərˈget/ v. ★★★ esquecer *They never forget to call me on my birthday.*

formality /fɔrˈmæləti/ n. ★ formalidade *The interview is just a formality.*

fortunate /ˈfɔrtʃənət/ adj. ★★ afortunado *Not everyone is as fortunate as we are.*

founder /ˈfaʊndər/ n. ★ fundador *He is one of the original founders of the Libertarian party.*

freedom /ˈfridəm/ n. ★★★ liberdade *The school gives students freedom of choice about what to wear.*

freshness n. frescor *I love feeling the freshness of early mornings.*

fried /fraɪd/ adj. ★ frito *Fried chicken is delicious, but not very healthy.*

friendly /ˈfren(d)li/ adj. ★★★ amigável *This dog has a friendly look.*

frontier /frʌnˈtɪr/ n. ★★ fronteira *Space is the final frontier.*

frozen /ˈfroʊz(ə)n/ adj. congelado *He loves having frozen yogurt for dessert.*

fruit /frut/ n. ★★★ fruta *Peaches are my favorite fruit.*

fulfill /fʊlˈfɪl/ v. ★★ preencher *The church fulfills a necessary role in this town.*

full /fʊl/ adj. ★★★ cheio *There is a box full of chocolates on the table.*

fully /ˈfʊli/ adv. ★★★ completamente *He was lying on the bed, fully dressed.*

funeral /ˈfjun(ə)rəl/ n. ★★ funeral *He went home to arrange his father's funeral.*

funny /ˈfʌni/ adj. ★★★ engraçado *I don't think that's funny.*

furniture /ˈfɜrnɪtʃər/ n. ★★★ móveis *His house is all decorated with antique furniture.*

furthermore /ˈfɜrðərˌmɔr/ adv. ★★ além disso *Mr. Brown has earned the respect of farmers everywhere. Furthermore, they know they can trust him.*

G

gain /geɪn/ v. n. ★★★ obter *The Green Party gains new supporters every year.*

game /geɪm/ n. ★★★ jogo, competição esportiva *We always watch volleyball games.*

garbage /ˈgɑrbɪdʒ/ n. ★ lixo *Throw the garbage into the trash can, please.*

gesture /ˈdʒestʃər/ n. ★★ gesto *Offering to drive us there was a very nice gesture.*

get /get/ v. ★★★ obter *Buy a movie ticket and get another on for free.*

get through phrasal verb passar por *The refugees will need help to get through the winter.*

give /gɪv/ v. ★★★ dar *Give me the car keys.*

give up phrasal verb desistir *Decide what you want and then don't give up until you've achieved it.*

glasses /ˈglɑsəz/ n. ★ óculos *My glasses are broken.*

go /goʊ/ v. ★★★ ir *We go to bed at 9 o'clock.*

go back phrasal verb voltar *I will go back to the house after the movie.*

goal /goʊl/ n. ★★★ objetivo, meta *Our goal is to provide a good standard of medical care.*

good /gʊd/ adj. ★★★ bom *Ivan is a good friend.*

goodwill /gʊdˈwɪl/ n. ★ boa vontade *As a gesture of goodwill, we agreed to do the work free of charge.*

grade /greɪd/ n. ★★ série *I am in the 6th grade.*

grain /greɪn/ n. ★★ grão *At night, I prefer to eat grains and salad.*

gray /greɪ/ adj. ★★★ cinza *The sky is really gray this afternoon.*

great /greɪt/ adj. ★★★ ótimo *Lucca is a great student.*

greenhouse gas /ˈgrinˌhaʊs gæs/ n. gás de efeito estufa *Greenhouse gases are partially responsible for the recent temperature increase.*

grooming /ˈgrumɪŋ/ n. higiene, tratamento *Dog grooming may include bathing and trimming.*

ground /graʊnd/ n. ★★★ chão *Do not leave your bag on the ground.*

grow /groʊ/ v. ★★★ crescer *That tree can grow to over 100 feet tall.*

grow up phrasal verb crescer *She's really starting to grow up now.*

guy /gaɪ/ n. ★★★ cara (informal), rapaz *Bob's a really nice guy.*

H

hair /her/ n. ★★★ cabelo *His hair is red and short.*

hairstyle /ˈherˌstaɪl/ n. ★ estilo de cabelo *Their hairstyle is really modern.*

ham /hæm/ n. ★ presunto *Ham and cheese sandwiches are a common snack among children.*

hand in phrasal verb entregar *Please hand in your keys when you leave the hotel.*

handle /ˈhænd(ə)l/ v. ★★★ lidar *Flight attendants are trained to handle difficult passengers.*

handsome /ˈhænsəm/ adj. ★★ bonito *Joe was tall, dark, and handsome.*

hang out phrasal verb sair *Jason and Eliseu hang out frequently.*

happen /ˈhæpən/ v. ★★★ acontecer *Bienal do Livro happens every two years.*

hard /hɑrd/ adj. ★★★ duro; difícil *This sofa is not comfortable; it is too hard.*

harmful /ˈhɑrmfəl/ adj. ★ danoso, nocivo The fungus is not harmful to humans.

hate /heɪt/ v. ★★★ odiar *I hate the smell of cigarettes.*

have to phrase ter de *We have to clean the table after eating.*

headline /ˈhedˌlaɪn/ n. ★★ manchete *The headlines today are about the elections.*

health /helθ/ n. ★★★ saúde *It is important to take care of your health.*

healthy /ˈhelθi/ adj. ★★★ saudável *Eating salad is a healthy habit.*

hear /hɪə(r)/ v. ★★★ ouvir *Can you hear that noise?*

hearing-impaired adj. deficiente auditivo *I have two hearing-impaired classmates.*

heart /hɑː(r)t/ n. ★★★ coração *The heart is one of the most important organs in our bodies.*

heat /hit/ v. n. ★★ aquecer, calor *Heat the oil gently in a large frying pan.*

heel /hil/ n. ★★ salto *These sandals have high heels.*

height /haɪt/ n. ★★★ altura What's your height?

help /help/ v. n. ★★★ ajudar; ajuda *I need help with my homework.*

helpful /'helpfəl/ adj. ★★ prestativo *If you're tired, caffeine can be helpful in low doses.*

hen /hen/ n. galinha *They have more than twenty hens on the farm.*

here /hɪr/ adv. ★★★ aqui *I live here in Natal.*

hero /'hɪroʊ/ n. ★★ herói *Elvis has been my hero since I was a little boy.*

hide /haɪd/ v. ★★★ esconder *I wanted to hide his present from him until his birthday.*

hiking /'haɪkɪŋ/ n. caminhada *Hiking is his favorite physical activity.*

hire /'haɪr/ v. ★★ contratar *I hired someone to paint the house.*

hit /hɪt/ v. ★★★ bater *Don't hit your brother!*

hold /hoʊld/ v. ★★★ segurar *Hold your breath and jump into the water.*

home /həʊm/ n. ★★★ lar, casa *What time are you coming home?* **homeless** sem teto **homemade** caseiro

homophobia /ˌhoʊmə'foʊbiə/ n. homofobia *In some countries, homophobia is considered a crime.*

horrible /'hɔrəb(ə)l/ adj. ★★ horrível *I've had a horrible day at work.*

horse /hɔː(r)s/ n. ★★★ cavalo *Riding horses is one of Paula's pastimes.*

hospitable /hɑ'spɪtəb(ə)l/ adj. hospitaleiro *We spent the weekend in a very hospitable environment.*

house /haʊs/ n. ★★★ casa *My house is the green one.*

how /haʊ/ adv. conj. ★★★ como *How much sugar do you want? How many olives do you want?*

huge /hjudʒ/ adj. ★★★ enorme *The band is huge in both Britain and the U.S.*

humanize /'hjuməˌnaɪz/ v. humanizar *The judge is making efforts to humanize the criminal justice system.*

humorous /'hjumərəs/ adj. ★ humorístico *This is not a soap opera; it is a humorous program.*

hunger /'hʌŋgər/ n. ★ fome *Hunger is still a problem for millions of people around the world.*

hungry /'hʌŋgri/ adj. ★★ faminto *I'm so hungry; I need to eat.*

husband /'hʌzbənd/ n. ★★★ marido *Carole's husband died last year.*

hut /hʌt/ n. ★★ cabana *They work in a beach hut.*

I

ice /aɪs/ n. ★★★ gelo *Ice covered most of the lake.*

idea /aɪ'diə/ n. ★★★ ideia *Your idea is great!*

identity /aɪ'dentəti/ n. ★★★ identidade *Do you have any proof of identity?*

if /ɪf/ conj. ★★★ se *Call me if you need anything.*

illustrate /'ɪləˌstreɪt/ v. ★★★ ilustrar *Miriam used examples to illustrate her point.*

impatient /ɪm'peɪʃ(ə)nt/ adj. ★ impaciente *After a couple of days, she was impatient to get back to work.*

impolite /ˌɪmpə'laɪt/ adj. ★ mal educado *It would be impolite to leave the party so early.*

importance /ɪm'pɔrt(ə)ns/ n. ★★★ importância *The issue has special importance to people in rural areas.*

improper /ɪm'prɑpər/ adj. impróprio *He had made improper suggestions to her.*

include /ɪn'klud/ v. ★★★ incluir *The batteries are not included in the toy.*

income /'ɪnˌkʌm/ n. ★★★ renda *Most of the villagers rely on farming for income.*

indigenous /ɪn'dɪdʒənəs/ adj. indígena *This is a preserved indigenous community.*

ingest /ɪn'dʒest/ v. ingerir *She ingested a significant amount of water when swimming.*

inhabitant /ɪn'hæbɪt(ə)nt/ n. ★★ habitante *The city's first inhabitants arrived in the 16th century.*

inherit /ɪn'herɪt/ v. ★★ herdar *Their children inherited a house and a factory.*

inner /'ɪnər/ adj. ★★★ interno, intrínseco *He reached into the inner pocket of his jacket.*

insensitive /ɪn'sensətɪv/ adj. insensível *He is totally insensitive to my feelings.*

inside /'ɪnˌsaɪd/ adj. adv. pron. ★★★ dentro *I always keep important papers locked inside my desk..*

inspiration /ˌɪnspɪ'reɪʃ(ə)n/ n. ★★ inspiração *Dreams are a rich source of inspiration for some writers.* **inspiring** inspirador

instead /ɪn'sted/ adv. ★★★ ao invés de *If you don't have olive oil, you can use sunflower oil instead.*

intelligent /ɪn'telɪdʒənt/ adj. ★★ inteligente *Is there intelligent life elsewhere in the universe?*

intention /ɪn'tenʃ(ə)n/ n. ★★★ intenção *We have no intention of giving up.*

interesting /'ɪntrəstɪŋ/ adj. ★★★ interessante *This new movie is very interesting.* **interest** interesse

interview /'ɪntərˌvju/ n. ★★★ entrevista *Justin Bieber's interview is at 4 o'clock.*

intonation /ˌɪntə'neɪʃ(ə)n/ n. ★ entonação *Pay attention to the correct intonation of these words.*

intrusion /ɪn'truʒ(ə)n/ n. ★ invasão *How do you deal with the constant intrusions of the media?*

irrational /ɪ'ræʃən(ə)l/ adj. irracional *The market's enthusiasm for high-tech stocks was irrational but understandable.*

island /'aɪlənd/ n. ★★★ ilha *The hotel is the best on the island.*

isolated /'aɪsəˌleɪtəd/ adj. ★ isolado *That bedroom is isolated from the rest of the house.*

issue /'ɪʃu/ n. ★★★ questão *It's a website devoted to environmental issues.*

J

January /'dʒænjuˌeri/ n. ★★★ janeiro *January is the first month of the year.*

jingle /'dʒɪŋg(ə)l/ n. mensagem publicitária musicada *That advertising has a jingle that sticks in your mind.*

job /dʒɒb/ n. ★★★ trabalho *Heloisa leaves her job at 6 o'clock.*

join /dʒɔɪn/ v. ★★★ unir-se a *Join the club and play the games.*

judge /dʒʌdʒ/ n. ★★★ juíz *The judge has the final word.*

jump /dʒʌmp/ v. ★★★ pular *The cat jumped up onto my lap.*

junk /dʒʌŋk/ adj. ★ porcaria *Not all sandwiches are junk food; some can be very healthy.*

K

karaoke /ˌkeri'oʊki/ n. karaokê *His birthday turned into a karaoke night.*

keep /kip/ v. ★★★ manter *Keep calm and carry on.*

kill /kɪl/ v. ★★★ matar *The nurse will give you something to kill the pain.*

kid /kɪd/ n. ★★★ criança *The kids are in the garden.*

kind /kaɪnd/ adj. ★★★ gentil, tipo **kind of** *The waiter was very kind to us.*

king /kɪŋ/ n. ★★★ rei *Oswald became king in 634.*

knee /ni/ n. ★★★ joelho *Bend your knees when you pick up heavy objects.*

know /nəʊ/ v. saber *I know how to draw a castle.*

knowledge /'nalɪdʒ/ n. ★★★ conhecimento *We had no knowledge of the incident.*

L

lamb /læm/ n. ★ cordeiro *We had roast lamb for dinner.*

last /læst/ v. adj. adv. ★★★ durar, último *My sister is on the last train to Brighton.*

late /leɪt/ adj. ★★★ tarde *She called to say she'd be late.*

later /'leɪtər/ adv. ★★★ mais tarde *I expect her home later.*

laugh /lɑːf/ v. n. ★★ rir, riso, risada *When I tell a joke, my brother laughs.*

law /lɔ/ n. ★★★ lei *It is against the law to smoke here.*

leading /'lidɪŋ/ adj. ★★★ principal, mais importante *He became a leading figure in the London art world.*

learn /lɜː(r)n/ v. ★★★ aprender *We learn English at school.*

least /list/ adj. adv. ★★★ menos, o menos *Troubles come when you least expect them.*

leather /'leðər/ n. ★★ couro *I don't wear leather shoes.*

leave /liːv/ v. ★★★ deixar, partir *Leave me alone.*

leisure /'liʒər/ n. ★★ lazer *I'm looking forward to more leisure time in my retirement.*

less /les/ adv. det. prep. pron. ★★★ menos *Put less water for me, please.*

let's /lets/ short form "let us" ★★★ vamos *Let's go to the movies this afternoon.*

letter /'letər/ n. ★★★ carta **letter paper** papel de carta *Laurie sometimes receives letters.*

lie /laɪ/ v. ★★★ mentir *She admitted lying to the police.*

life /laɪf/ n. ★★★ vida *Your life starts when you are born and finishes when you die.*

light /laɪt/ n. adj. ★★★ luz, claridade; leve, claro *Turn on the lights; it is really dark in here.*

like /laɪk/ v. gostar *Andy and Andrew like bowling.*

listen /'lɪs(ə)n/ v. ★★★ ouvir *Listen to your teacher.*

listener /'lɪs(ə)nər/ n. ★ ouvinte *The show attracted over 3 million listeners in its first week.*

literature /'lɪt(ə)rətʃər/ n. ★★★ literatura *She is studying German language and literature.*

locally /'loʊk(ə)li/ adv. ★★ localmente *Most of the fruit they sell is grown locally.*

located /loʊ'keɪtɪd/ adj. (nunca antes de substantivo) ★★ localizado *The hotel is located in downtown Hartford.*

lose /luːz/ v. ★★★ perder *They train so hard because they cannot lose this game.*

lottery /'lɑtəri/ n. ★ loteria *She won a million dollars in the lottery.*

love /lʌv/ n. v. ★★★ amor, amar *Dogs love playing.*

low-fat adj. com pouca gordura *This low-fat margarine is really tasty.*

luxury /'lʌɡʒ(ə)ri/ n. ★ luxo *They live a life of absolute luxury.*

M

magazine /'mæɡəˌzin/ n. ★★★ revista *Seventeen is a magazine for teenagers.*

main /meɪn/ adj. ★★★ principal *The teacher's room is in the main building.*

major /'meɪdʒər/ adj. ★★★ maior *Age is a major factor affecting chances of employment.*

make /meɪk/ v. ★★★ fazer *Let's make a cake.*

make sure phrase assegurar-se *I just wanted to make sure you knew where to go.*

mall /mɔl/ n. ★★ centro de compras *We can ride a bike or go to the shopping mall.*

manage /'mænɪdʒ/ v. ★★★ conseguir; obter sucesso; gerenciar *He manages the family business.*

management /'mænɪdʒmənt/ n. ★★★ gerenciamento *The heart of effective management is communication.*

manifesto /ˌmænɪ'festoʊ/ n. manifesto *They wrote a manifesto against the last government decisions.*

March /martʃ/ n. ★★★ março *The concert is on March 29th.*

market /'markət/ n. ★★★ mercado *Europe is the main market for our cars.*

marriage /'merɪdʒ/ n. ★★★ casamento *Too many marriages end in divorce.*

marry /'meri/ v. ★★★ casar *When two people marry, they enter into a contract with each other.*

match /mætʃ/ v. ★★★ ligar, conectar *Match the words to their definitions.*

matter /'mætər/ v. ★★★ importar, ser importante *People need to realize that education matters.*

May /me□/ n. ★★★ maio *They were married on May 17th.*

maybe /'meɪbi/ adj. ★★★ talvez *Maybe I am getting the flu; I feel hot.*

meal /mil/ n. ★★★ refeição *Breakfast is the first meal we have in a day.*

mean /min/ v. ★★★ significar *What does "book" mean?*

meaningful /'minɪŋfəl/ adj. ★ significativo *The students had a meaningful discussion.*

meat /mit/ n. ★★★ carne *Vegetarians do not eat meat, chicken, or fish.*

mechanic /mə'kænɪk/ n. ★ mecânico *My father is a mechanic, so he fixes cars.*

medicine /'medɪsɪn/ n. ★★ medicina; medicamento *You have to take the medicine three timesa day.*

meet /mit/ v. ★★★ encontrar, conhecer *Sam meets his friends every Friday afternoon.*

meme /mim/ n. meme *"Menos Luiza, que está no Canadá." was a very popular meme.*

memorable /'mem(ə)rəb(ə)l/ adj. memorável *The romantic evening cruise will be a memorable experience.*

mention /'menʃ(ə)n/ n. ★★★ mencionar; menção *He didn't mention her all evening.*

message /'mesɪdʒ/ n. ★★★ mensagem **instant messaging** *There is a message for you in your notebook.*

middle /'mɪd(ə)l/ n. ★★★ meio *Their dog sleeps between them in the middle of the bed.*

might /maɪt/ mod. v. ★★★ (indica possibilidade remota) *You never know what might happen in the future.*

milk /mɪlk/ n. ★★★ leite *Ray drinks chocolate milk.*

mimic /'mɪmɪk/ n. mímica *If you do not know how to say that in English, you can use mimics to express yourself.*

mind /maɪnd/ n. v. ★★★ mente, importar-se *I need a walk to clear my mind.*

minute /'mɪnɪt/ n. ★★★ minuto *I'll meet you downstairs in ten minutes.*

miss /mɪs/ v. ★★★ perder; sentir saudades *I had to miss a week of school.*

mistake /mɪ'steɪk/ n. ★★★ erro *I won't make the same mistake again!*

mohawk /'moʊˌhɔk/ n. moicano (penteado) *The mohawk was a trendy hairstyle in the 1980s.*

money /'mʌni/ n. ★★★ dinheiro *I need money to buy popcorn.*

monkey /'mʌŋki/ n. ★ macaco *Most monkeys love eating bananas.*

mood /mud/ n. ★★★ humor *Your mood can be affected by your hormones.*

more /mɔr/ adv. det. pron. ★★★ mais *I want more rice, please.*

morning /'mɔrnɪŋ/ n. ★★★ manhã *I wake up at 6 in the morning.*

motivation /ˌmoʊtɪ'veɪʃ(ə)n/ n. ★★ motivação *Their real motivation is to make a profit.*

move /muv/ v. ★★★ mover, mudar-se *Our neighbors will move to another city.*

moviemaker /'muviˌmeɪkər/ n. cineasta *Wilma's son is a moviemaker.*

mud /mʌd/ n. ★★ lama *Rain turned the road to mud.*

music /ˈmjuzɪk/ n. ★★★ música *What's your favorite kind of music?*

must /mʌst/ mod. v. ★★★ dever *You must do your homework.*

N

napkin /ˈnæpkɪn/ n. guardanapo *Use your napkin to clean your mouth.*

nation /ˈneɪʃ(ə)n/ n. ★★★ nação *We want the government to serve the whole nation.*

nature /ˈneɪtʃər/ n. ★★★ natureza *Barone's interest was in nature, wildlife, and birds.*

necessary /ˈnesəs(ə)ri/ adj. ★★★ necessário *It is necessary to close your eyes to sleep.*

need /nid/ v. ★★★ precisar *We need milk to make this cake.*

neglected adj. negligenciado *The garden was neglected and overgrown.*

neither /ˈniðər/ conj.pron. ★★★ nem *"I don't feel like going to the party." "Me neither."*

never /ˈnevər/ adv. ★★★ nunca *You should never cross when the light is red.*

newspaper /ˈnuzˌpeɪpər/ n. ★★★ jornal, periódico *Celia reads the newspaper every morning.*

next /nekst/ adj. adv. det. pron. ★★★ próximo; do lado *I sit next to him.*

nice /naɪs/ adj. ★★★ legal *He is a nice teacher.*

night /naɪt/ n. ★★★ noite *Good night, see you tomorrow.*

nostalgic /nɑˈstældʒɪk/ adj. nostálgico *A lot of adults feel nostalgic about their childhood.*

November /noʊˈvembər/ n. ★★★ novembro *The play opens on November 15th.*

O

oatmeal /ˈoʊtˌmil/ n. mingau de aveia *Charlie has oatmeal for breakfast.*

obligation /ˌɑblɪˈgeɪʃ(ə)n/ n. ★★★ obrigação *The firm has an obligation to its clients.*

obituary /əˈbɪtʃuˌeri/ n. obituário *Ronald's family published a beautiful obituary in the newspaper after his death.*

October /ɑkˈtoʊbər/ n. ★★★ outubro *We're going to Boston in October.*

offer /ˈɔfər/ v. n. ★★★ oferecer, oferta **special offer** oferta especial, promoção *Today, the snack bar has a special offer.*

often /ˈɔf(ə)n/ adv. ★★★ frequente, frequentemente *Leonard often goes to the cinema.*

oil /ɔɪl/ n. ★★★ óleo *Cook the chicken in some oil.*

old /oʊld/ adj. ★★★ velho *My teacher is not very old.*

once /wʌns/ adv. ★★★ uma vez; uma vez que *Once I watched a football game in a stadium.*

only /ˈəʊnli/ adv. ★★★ só, somente *This toilet is only for women.*

opinion /əˈpɪnjən/ n. ★★★ opinião *What is your opinion of her latest novel?*

opposite /ˈɑpəzɪt/ adj. ★★★ oposto, contrário a *This proposal will have the opposite effect from the previous one.*

order /ˈɔː(r)də(r)/ v. n. ★★★ pedir; pedido, ordem *Let's order some pizza for dinner.*

organic /ɔrˈgænɪk/ adj. ★ orgânico *Is this milk organic?*

outdoor /aʊtˈdɔr/ adj. ★ externo *Julio likes outdoor activities such as walking and camping.*

outside /ˌaʊtˈsaɪd/ adj. adv. prep. ★★★ externo; do lado de fora; fora *They will build a factory outside town.*

oven /ˈʌv(ə)n/ n. ★★ forno *Bake for 25 minutes, then reduce the oven temperature.*

overcome /ˌoʊvərˈkʌm/ v. ★★ superar *Jimmy overcame his difficulties to graduate.*

oversized /ˈoʊvərˌsaɪzd/ adj. maior do que de costume *The sandwiches there are oversized; I can never finish them.*

own /əʊn/ adj. pron. ★★★ próprio *Dan has his own bedroom.*

P

pack /pæk/ n. ★★★ embalagem *We want a pack of fries.*

painter /ˈpeɪntər/ n. ★★ pintor *The gallery is showing the work of abstract painters.*

painting /ˈpeɪntɪŋ/ n. ★★★ pintura; quadro *He does jobs for me like painting and decorating.*

pamphlet /ˈpæmflət/ n. panfleto *A pamphlet is one of the most common forms of advertising.*

paper /ˈpeɪpər/ n. ★★★ papel *Write your name on a piece of paper.*

paradise /ˈperəˌdaɪs/ n. ★ paraíso *With 30 bookstores in this neighborhood alone, San Francisco is a book lover's paradise.*

park /pɑrk/ n. ★★★ parque *This park closes at 8 o'clock.*

part-time adj. ★★ meio-período *Loli studies in the morning and has a part-time job in the afternoon.*

party /ˈpɑrti/ n. ★★★ festa **house party** festa em casa *My friend is throwing a house party tonight.*

pass around phrasal verb circular *The photos were passed around for each of them to have a look at.*

pasta /ˈpɑstə/ n. ★ massa *Ravioli is Celi's favorite kind of pasta.*

pay /peɪ/ v. ★★★ pagar **pay attention** prestar atenção *Pay attention to the teacher's instructions.*

peacemaker /ˈpisˌmeɪkər/ n. pacificador *The ex-president has been honored as a peacemaker.*

pendant /ˈpendənt/ n. pingente *Her necklace is decorated with pendants.*

person /ˈpɜː(r)s(ə)n/ n. ★★★ pessoa (pessoas) **people** pessoas *Barack Obama is a famous person all over the world.*

per /pɜr/ prep. ★★★ por **per week** por semana *Aryane studies five hours per week.*

pesticide /ˈpestɪˌsaɪd/ n. pesticida *Organic farmers do not use pesticide on their crops.*

pet /pet/ n. ★★ animal de estimação *He has a fish as a pet.*

petition /pəˈtɪʃ(ə)n/ n. ★★ petição *More than 300 villagers have signed a petition against the construction project.*

philosophy /fɪˈlɑsəfi/ n. ★★★ filosofia *Philosophy was invented by the Greeks.*

photograph /ˈfoʊtəˌgræf/ n. ★★★ fotografia **photo album** álbum de fotos *Macy's grandfather takes beautiful photographs.*

physicist /ˈfɪzɪsɪst/ n. físico *Newton was one of the most famous physicists ever.*

pick /pɪk/ v. ★★★ pegar, escolher *Pick the T-shirt you prefer, and I will take the other one.*

picnic /ˈpɪknɪk/ n. ★ piquenique *Let's have a picnic in the park.*

picture /ˈpɪktʃər/ n. ★★★ ilustração, foto *Look at the pictures on page 56.*

pig /pɪg/ n. ★★ porco *There are more than twenty pigs on that farm.*

piglet /ˈpɪglət/ n. leitão *That pig had two piglets last night.*

pineapple /ˈpaɪnˌæp(ə)l/ n. abacaxi *Maria and Hélio always choose the pineapple ice cream.*

place /pleɪs/ n. ★★★ lugar, local *My room is my favorite place.*

plan /plæn/ v. n. ★★★ planejar; plano *My boss is planning to retire at 50.*

plant /plænt/ v. n. ★★ plantar; planta *I planted a small apple tree in the garden.*

plate /pleɪt/ n. ★★★ prato *Wash these plates and glasses, please.*

play /pleɪ/ v. n. ★★★ jogar, tocar, atuar; peça de teatro *Let's play volleyball at the beach.*

player /ˈpleɪər/ n. ★★★ jogador; tocador *Ronaldo used to be a soccer player.*

plywood /ˈplaɪˌwʊd/ n. compensado *These walls are made of plywood.*

poem /ˈpoʊəm/ n. ★★★ poema *I wrote a poem about my childhood.*

poetry /ˈpoʊətri/ n. ★★ poesia *Do you prefer prose or poetry?*

political /pəˈlɪtɪk(ə)l/ adj. ★★★ político *Environmental changes are political issues.*

poll /poʊl/ n. ★★ pesquisa *A recent poll indicated that most people opposed the changes.*

pollution /pəˈluʃ(ə)n/ n. ★★★ poluição *Pollution is a major problem in big cities.*

pomegranate /ˈpɒmɪˌɡrænət/ n. romã *Pomegranate is how we say romã in English.*

pool /pul/ n. ★★★ poça (d'água) *I saw some water collected in a little pool at the bottom of the cliff.*

poor /pʊr/ adj. ★★★ pobre *We were very poor and could barely afford the necessities of life.*

pork /pɔrk/ n. ★ carne de porco *Do you eat pork?*

possibility /ˌpɑsəˈbɪləti/ n. ★★★ possibilidade *Another possibility is that we'll go to Mexico instead.*

possible /ˈpɑsəb(ə)l/ adj. ★★★ possível *The task will not be possible without access to the Internet.*

power /ˈpaʊər/ n. ★★★ poder *He has an amazing power of concentration.*

practice /ˈpræktɪs/ v. n. ★★★ praticar; prática *Practice leads you to perfection.*

prediction /prɪˈdɪkʃ(ə)n/ n. ★★ previsão *The government maintained its prediction that inflation will hold to 8.5% this year.*

prejudice /ˈpredʒədɪs/ n. ★★ preconceito *We want to overcome prejudice against women in politics.*

pretty /ˈprɪti/ adj. ★★ bonita *He has a very pretty wife.*

prevent /prɪˈvent/ v. ★★★ prevenir *Regular cleaning may help prevent infection.*

price /praɪs/ n. ★★★ preço *Students don't have to pay regular price; they get a discount.*

principle /ˈprɪnsəp(ə)l/ n. ★★★ princípio *Excellent customer service should be our guiding principle.*

print /prɪnt/ v. n. ★★★ imprimir; impressão *Print six copies of this paper.*

probably /ˈprɑbəbli/ adv. ★★★ provavelmente *I'll cook a meal, probably lasagna or something.*

product /ˈprɑdəkt/ n. ★★★ produto *You can complain if the product does not work.*

prohibition /ˌproʊəˈbɪʃ(ə)n/ n. ★ proibição *There is an explicit prohibition against smoking and drinking in here.*

promote /prəˈmoʊt/ v. ★★★ promover *They are promoting a new book at the bookshop.*

prompt /prɑmpt/ n. breve nota *Use these prompts to form the text.*

proofread /ˈprufˌrid/ v. revisar (textos) *You should proofread your compositions before handing them in.*

proper /ˈprɑpər/ adj. ★★ apropriado *That's not the proper way to do it!*

propose /prəˈpoʊz/ v. ★★ propor *I propose going to an early movie and having dinner afterward.*

proposition /ˌprɑpəˈzɪʃ(ə)n/ n. ★★ proposta *I have a business proposition to put to you.*

publish /ˈpʌblɪʃ/ v. ★★★ publicar *They publish story books.*

puppy /ˈpʌpi/ n. ★ filhote *Niko is the name of our new puppy dog.*

put down phrasal verb sacrificar (animal) *We're probably going to have the cat put down next week.*

Q

quote /kwoʊt/ v. n. ★★★ citar; citação *Some people quote famous writers on Facebook.*

R

race /reɪs/ n. ★★★ raça *We do not discriminate on the basis of race or gender.*

racism /ˈreɪˌsɪzəm/ n. ★ racismo *They promised to continue the struggle against racism.*

rain /reɪn/ v. n. ★★★ chover; chuva *Outside the rain continued to fall steadily.*

raise /reɪz/ v. ★★★ levantar *Raise your hand to ask a question.*

raised /reɪzd/ adj. ★ levantado, mais alto *The larger goods are displayed on raised platforms.*

rate /reɪt/ v. avaliar; graduar *Many voters rate the environment as the number one issue.*

read /rid/ v. ★★★ ler *Read the question and answer in your notebook.* **reader** leitor **reading** leitura

reader /ˈridər/ n. ★★★ leitor *Cecilia is a compulsive reader.*

reason /ˈriz(ə)n/ n. ★★★ razão *The police asked her the reason for her visit.*

receive /rɪˈsiv/ v. ★★★ receber *We have not received your letter.*

recommend /ˌrekəˈmend/ v. ★★★ recomendar *I recommend that you buy a more powerful computer.*

recover /rɪˈkʌvər/ v. ★★★ recuperar-se *Julio is recovering well from his foot surgery.*

recyclable /riˈsaɪkləb(ə)l/ adj. reciclável *These plastic bottles are recyclable.*

reflect /rɪˈflekt/ v. ★★★ refletir *The mirror reflects the sunbeams.*

refrigerated /rɪˈfrɪdʒəˌreɪt/ adj. refrigerado *We keep the candy in a refrigerated room.*

regardless /rɪˈɡardləs/ adv. ★★ independentemente de *Regardless of his formal education, he is a genuine artist.*

relationship /rɪˈleɪʃ(ə)nˌʃɪp/ n. ★★★ relacionamento *They are in a serious relationship.*

remember /rɪˈmembər/ v. ★★★ lembrar *Remember to call me when you get there.*

renewable /rɪˈnuəb(ə)l/ adj. renovável *Wind is a renewable source of energy.*

repetitive /rɪˈpetətɪv/ adj. repetitivo *This song is too repetitive; change it.*

replace /rɪˈpleɪs/ v. ★★★ substituir *Roque replaced Denis in the second round of the game.*

report /rɪˈpɔrt/ v. n. ★★★ relatório; reportar *We have to write a report about the accident.*

require /rɪˈkwaɪr/ v. ★★★ requerer, pedir *Working with children requires a great deal of patience.*

rescue /ˈreskju/ v. n. ★★ resgatar; resgate *The team rescued the dog from the burning building.*

residue /ˈrezɪdu/ n. resíduo *There is some orange residue at the bottom of the bottle.*

resource /ˈriˌsɔrs/ n. ★★★ fonte, recurso *Songs are a great resource for vocabulary.*

respectful /rɪˈspektf(ə)l/ adj. respeitoso *He is a very respectful gentleman.*

responsibility /rɪˌspɑnsəˈbɪləti/ n. ★★★ responsabilidade *Doing the homework is the responsibility of the student.* **responsible** responsável

retire /rɪˈtaɪr/ v. ★★ aposentar-se *He plans to retire next year.*

review /rɪˈvju/ n. ★★★ resenha *There was a good review about that movie.*

rewrite /ˌriˈraɪt/ v. ★ reescrever *Rewrite the sentences using the words from the box.*

rhyme /raɪm/ n. ★ rima *Can you think of a rhyme for "hat"?*

rhythm /ˈrɪðəm/ n. ★★ ritmo *Let's dance to the rhythm of the song.*

rice /raɪs/ n. ★★ arroz *Harry eats rice and beans every day.*

rich /rɪtʃ/ adj. ★★★ rico *His invention has made him a rich man.*

right /raɪt/ adv. ★★★ certo, direito *Our teacher is the one on the right of the photo.*

road /roʊd/ n. ★★★ rua *They live on Abbey Road.*

robbery /ˈrɑbəri/ n. ★ roubo *There was a robbery in the neighborhood last night.*

rock 'n' roll n. ★ rock *Rock 'n' roll is a very popular kind of music.*

room /rum/ n. ★★★ quarto, sala, espaço *There is plenty of room in this garden.*

rooster /'rustər/ n. galo *The rooster crows at 5 o'clock in the morning every day.*

S

sad /sæd/ adj. ★★★ triste *That is a sad story.*

safe /seɪf/ adj. ★★★ seguro *It is safe to use banks through the Internet.* **safety** segurança

saggy /'sægi/ adj. caída *Some teens like wearing saggy pants.*

salary /'sæləri/ n. ★★ salário *Oliver receives his salary once a month.*

salt /sɔlt/ n. ★★ sal *You do not have to add salt to food.*

salty /'sɔlti/ adj. salgado *This rice is too salty.*

same /seɪm/ adj. adv. pron. ★★★ mesmo *We have the same name: we are both called Raj.*

satisfied /'sætɪs,faɪd/ adj. ★ satisfeito *Honestly, some people are never satisfied!*

say /seɪ/ v. ★★★ dizer *Don't just stand there! Say something!*

scared /skerd/ adj. ★★★ assustado *Joana is scared of scorpions.*

scary /'skeri/ adj. ★ assustador *That was a really scary movie.*

scholarship /'skɑlər,ʃɪp/ n. ★ bolsa de estudos *She got a scholarship to the university.*

school /skul/ n. ★★★ escola **school grade** ano escolar **school office** secretaria da escola *What is your school grade?*

schoolyard /'skul,jɑrd/ n. pátio da escola *The kids are playing in the schoolyard.*

scientist /'saɪəntɪst/ n. ★★★ cientista *Pasteur was an important scientist.*

scooter /'skutər/ n. motocicleta *He goes to school on a scooter.*

sculpture /'skʌlptʃər/ n. ★★ escultura *Rodin made a sculpture called "The Thinker".*

season /'siz(ə)n/ n. ★★★ estação *The year is divided into four seasons.*

seasonal /'siz(ə)nəl/ adj. sazonal *The tomato production is seasonal.*

second /'sekənd/ numb. ★★★ segundo *The second prize is a bicycle.*

see /si/ v. ★★★ ver *I love to see the sun rising.*

seek /sik/ v. ★★★ procurar *I am seeking someone to share the bills.*

sell /sel/ v. ★★★ vender *They sell movie tickets is this store.*

send /send/ v. ★★★ enviar *Send your photo by email.*

senseless /'sensləs/ adj. sem sentido *When he is sleeping, he says senseless things.*

September /sep'tembər/ n. ★★★ setembro *In the UK, the school year starts in September.*

service /'sɜrvɪs/ n. ★★★ serviço *This gas pump is out of service. Please use the other pump.*

sexism /'sek,sɪzəm/ n. sexismo *Sexism is a kind of prejudice.*

shall /ʃæl/ modal ★★★ poder *Shall we go now?*

shape /ʃeɪp/ n. v. ★★★ forma; formatar *This box has a square shape.*

share /ʃer/ v. ★★★ dividir *Let's share this piece of cake.*

sheep /ʃip/ n. ★★ ovelha *Count sheep until you fall asleep.*

shelter /'ʃeltər/ n. ★★ abrigo *I took the stray dog to a shelter.*

shirt /ʃɜrt/ n. ★★★ camisa **soccer shirt** camisa de futebol *I have a soccer shirt collection.*

shock /ʃɑk/ v. n. ★★★ chocar; choque *He went into shock when he found out about her death.*

short /ʃɔrt/ adj. ★★★ curto *Henry's hair is short.*

shortage /'ʃɔrtɪdʒ/ n. ★★ racionamento *We have to be prepared for water shortages during the summer.*

should /ʃʊd/ mod. v. ★★★ deveria *We all should study before the exam.*

show /ʃoʊ/ v. ★★★ mostrar, apresentar *Show me your cards.*

shrimp /ʃrɪmp/ n. camarão *I will make a shrimp casserole.*

shut /ʃʌt/ v. ★★★ fechar *Shut the door, please.*

sign language n. linguagem de sinais *Sign language is an effective way of communication.*

signature /'sɪgnətʃər/ n. ★★ assinatura *We have to check his signature with his identity card.*

simply /'sɪmpli/ adv. ★★★ simplesmente *He is simply the best singer ever.*

sing /sɪŋ/ v. ★★★ cantar *Aretha sings in a jazz band.* **singer** cantor

singer /'sɪŋər/ n. ★★ cantor *He is a popular Brazilian singer.*

single /'sɪŋg(ə)l/ adj. ★★★ solteiro *Debra's father is a single parent.*

size /saɪz/ n. ★★★ tamanho *My T-shirt size is extra large.*

slave /sleɪv/ n. ★★ escravo *Having a slave should be considered a crime.*

slavery /'sleɪv(ə)ri/ n. escravidão *Slavery should be prohibited in all countries.*

sleep /slip/ v. ★★★ dormir *Children sleep more hours than adults.*

slide /slaɪd/ n. escorregador *We love playing on the slide at the park.*

slogan /'sloʊgən/ n. ★ slogan *That slogan is hard to forget.*

small /smɔl/ adj. ★★★ pequeno *I have a small doll called Poppy.*

smelly /'smeli/ adj. fedido *That cheese is smelly!*

soap opera /soʊp 'ɑp(ə)rə/ n. novela *It is common to watch soap operas in Brazil.*

soil /sɔɪl/ n. ★★★ solo *Let's plant these seeds in the soil.*

something /'sʌmθɪŋ/ pron. ★★★ algo *I want something to eat.*

sometimes /'sʌmtaɪmz/ adv. ★★★ às vezes *Sometimes I study, sometimes I play sports.*

soon /sun/ adv. ★★★ logo *He will soon be here.*

sound /saʊnd/ n. ★★★ som **sound effect** efeito sonoro *The sound of rain calms her down.*

soup /sup/ n. ★★ sopa *Mafalda does not like soup.*

source /sɔrs/ n. ★★★ fonte *Sugar is a great source of energy.*

sovereignty /'sɑvrənti/ n. ★ soberania *The country's sovereignty is in danger.*

spam /spæm/ n. spam *I hate when I receive spam in my email.*

speak /spik/ v. ★★★ falar *Vicky speaks Portuguese and Italian.*

specialized /'speʃ(ə)l,aɪzd/ adj. ★ especializado *He specialized in Greek literature in college.*

speech /spitʃ/ n. ★★★ fala, discurso *The queen made a wonderful speech in reply.*

spelling /'spelɪŋ/ n. ★ grafia *What's the correct spelling of this word?*

spend /spend/ v. ★★★ gastar *He spends a lot on food.*

spread /spred/ v. ★★★ espalhar *Let's spread the good news.*

spring /sprɪŋ/ n. ★★★ primavera *In Brazil, spring starts in September.*

square /skwer/ n. ★★★ quadrado; praça *The garden has flower beds that form a perfect square.*

staff /stæf/ n. ★★★ pessoal *The restaurant staff is not complete today.*

stare /ster/ v. ★★★ encarar *It is rude to stare at people on the streets.*

start /stɑrt/ v. ★★★ começar *The game starts at 5 o'clock.*

statue /'stætʃu/ n. ★★ estátua *There is a statue of the poet in the city square.*

stay /steɪ/ v. ★★★ ficar *I stay in school until 1 o´clock.*

stop /stɑp/ v. ★★★ parar *Stop talking and breathe.*

storm /stɔrm/ n. ★★ tempestade *A storm hit the coast of Florida this morning.*

story /'stɔri/ n. ★★★ história *Ivy likes reading stories.*

stray /streɪ/ adj. perdido, sem casa *We found this stray dog last night.*

street /strit/ n. ★★★ rua *Fourth Street is very dangerous at night.*

strict /strɪkt/ adj. rígido *He's quite a strict coach, but we all like him.*

succeed /sək'sid/ v. ★★★ ter sucesso *We all want to make the peace process succeed.*

success /sək'ses/ n. ★★★ sucesso *A hit is a momentaneous success.*

such /sʌtʃ/ det. pron. ★★★ tal *He is such a nice friend!*

suffer /'sʌfər/ v. ★★★ sofrer *She suffered from depression for most of her adult life.*

sugary /'ʃʊgəri/ adj. açucarado *His songs are too sugary for me!*

summarize /'sʌmə,raɪz/ v. ★ resumir *Summarize the text in three sentences.*

summer /'sʌmər/ n. ★★★ verão *This room is cold even in summer.*

sunlight /'sʌn,laɪt/ n. ★★ luz do sol *Plants need sunlight to grow.*

supermarket /'supər,markət/ n. ★★ supermercado *There is a supermarket on the corner.*

supportive /sə'pɔrtɪv/ adj. que dá apoio, compreensivo *My boss was very supportive when I was sick.*

sure /ʃʊr/ adj. ★★★ claro, certo *I am sure he is in school.*

surgeon /'sɜrdʒən/ n. ★★ cirurgião *His aunt is a surgeon.*

surgery /'sɜrdʒəri/ n. ★★★ cirurgia *The surgery will happen next week.*

surprise /sər'praɪz/ n. ★★★ surpresa *It was a nice surprise when they arrived.*

survive /sər'vaɪv/ v. ★★★ sobreviver *Paula survived the accident.*

sustainable /sə'steɪnəb(ə)l/ adj. sustentável *We all should work for a more sustainable world.*

sweet /swit/ adj. n. ★★★ doce *This tea is too sweet; I can't drink it!*

swim /swɪm/ v. ★★ nadar *We love to swim in rivers.*

swimming pool n. piscina *There is a heated indoor swimming pool in that house.*

switch /swɪtʃ/ v. ★★★ trocar *He was accused of switching price tags.*

T

tablecloth /'teɪb(ə)l,klɑθ/ n. toalha de mesa *Please, bring me the red and white tablecloth.*

take /teɪk/ v. ★★★ tomar, tirar, levar **take care** cuidar **take a photo** tirar uma foto *Take care of the plants while I'm gone.*

time off n. tempo livre *I think I'll take some time off next week.*

talk /tɔk/ v. ★★★ falar *Talk to a classmate about your favorite hobbies.*

target /'tɑrgət/ n. ★★★ alvo *Teenagers are the target audience of this campaign.*

taste /teɪst/ n. ★★★ gosto, sabor *His taste in clothing is very expensive.*

teach /titʃ/ v. ★★★ ensinar *My brother and my uncle teach at the same school.*

teacher /'tiːtʃə(r)/ n. ★★★ professor **teacher's room** sala dos professores *During the break, the teachers have coffee in the teacher's room.*

teenager /'tin,eɪdʒər/ n. ★★ adolescente *Lee is fourteen; he is a teenager.*

tell /tel/ v. ★★★ dizer *Tell me the truth.*

terrarium /tə'reriəm/ n. terrarium *We grow three different kinds of plants in our terrarium.*

territory /'terə,tɔri/ n. ★★ território *The government plans to set aside indigenous territories.*

testimonial /,testə'moʊniəl/ n. testemunho *My friends write testimonials on my social network page.*

than /ðæn/ conj.prep. ★★★ do que (comparativo) *He is taller than me.*

theater /'θiətər/ n. ★★★ teatro **theater play** peça de teatro *Othello is a famous theater play by Shakespeare.*

theme park n. parque de diversões *There are great attractions in that theme park.*

then /ðen/ adj. adv. ★★★ então, em seguida *I brush my teeth, and then I go to bed.*

thick /θɪk/ adj. ★★★ espesso *This mango juice is really thick.*

think /θɪŋk/ v. ★★★ pensar *It is good to think before speaking.*

third /θɜrd/ numb. terceiro *Monique is the third of five children.*

through /θru/ adj.adv.prep. ★★★ por entre, por meio de *I can see through that window.*

thought /θɔt/ n. ★★★ pensamento, ideia *You should try to control your negative thoughts.*

thought-provoking /'θɔt prə,voʊkɪŋ/ adj. instigante *His ideas are quite thought-provokng.*

thus /ðʌs/ adv. assim, dessa forma *No decision had been made, and thus the situation remained unclear.*

ticket /'tɪkɪt/ n. ★★★ entrada, convite, bilhete *I have two tickets for the play.*

time /taɪm/ n. ★★★ tempo *We have time for a coffee.*

tip /tɪp/ n. ★★★ dica *Can you give me tips about the city?*

tired /'taɪrd/ adj. cansado *It is midnight and Pete is not tired yet.*

title /'taɪt(ə)l/ n. ★★★ título *Write a title for your composition.*

together /tə'geðər/ adv. ★★★ junto *We go to our English classes together.*

tomorrow /tə'mɔroʊ/ adv. ★★★ amanhã *Today is Thursday; tomorrow is Friday.*

tone /təʊn/ n. ★★★ tom *The positive tone of the evening had changed completely.*

too /tu/ adv. ★★★ também (usado no fim da frase) *You love me and I love you too.*

touch /tʌtʃ/ v. ★★★ tocar *Stretch your arms and try to touch your toes.*

tournament /'tɜrnəmənt/ n. ★★ campeonato *We will watch the tennis tournament on TV.*

towards /tɔrdz/ prep. ★★★ em direção a *Can the police clock your speed if they are driving towards you?*

town /taʊn/ n. ★★★ cidade *We live in a small town called Sombrio.*

train /treɪn/ n. ★★★ trem *This train leaves at midnight.*

trash /træʃ/ n. ★ lixo *This is trash, put it in the trash can.*

travel /'træv(ə)l/ v. ★★★ viajar *Let's travel to Maceió.*

tray /treɪ/ n. ★★ bandeja, travessa *The cups are on the tray.*

treat /trit/ v. ★★★ tratar *You should treat older people nicely.*

tree /tri/ n. ★★★ árvore *Let's rest under the tree.*

trip /trɪp/ n. ★★★ viagem *This trip will take about seven hours.*

truth /truθ/ n. ★★★ verdade *Please, tell me the truth.*

try /traɪ/ v. ★★★ tentar *They will try to learn Chinese!*

be turning phrase vai fazer (aniversário) *Felipe is turning eleven on Saturday.*

twice twaɪs/ adv. ★★★ duas vezes *I have swimming classes twice a week.*

type /taɪp/ v. n. ★★★ digitar, tipo *What type of food do you like?*

typo /'taɪpoʊ/ n. erro de digitação *There are no typos in this text.*

typography /taɪ'pagrəfi/ n. tipografia *Typography is an art.*

U

underline /,ʌndər'laɪn/ v. ★★ sublinhar *Underline the answers in the text.*

understand /ˌʌndər'stænd/ v. ★★★ entender *Do you understand the question?*

underwater /ˌʌndər'wɔtər/ adj. subaquática *Diving is an underwater sport.*

unhappy /ʌn'hæpi/ adj. ★★ infeliz *Her father was a desperately unhappy man.*

unhealthy /ʌn'helθi/ adj. pouco saudável *Your skin looks pale and unhealthy.*

until /ən'tɪl/ conj. prep. ★★★ até *I will stay here until you sleep.*

use /juz/ v. ★★★ usar *Use a pen to write your answers.*

used to /'just tu/ modal ★★★ costumava *Leo and Any used to have lunch together every day.*

usually /'juʒuəli/ adv. ★★★ geralmente *My brother usually washes his car at home.*

V

vacation /veɪ'keɪʃ(ə)n/ n. ★★ férias *I only get one week of vacation per year in this job.*

vacuum cleaner n. aspirador de pó *We do not have a vacuum cleaner at home.*

valuable /'væljəb(ə)l/ adj. ★★★ valioso *The necklace is not very valuable.*

vegetable /'vedʒ(ə)təb(ə)l/ n. ★★★ vegetal *Lettuce is a common vegetable in salads.* **vegetarian** vegetariano

vegetarian /ˌvedʒə'teriən/ n. adj. vegetariano *Rachel is vegetarian; she does not eat any kind of meat.*

verse /vɜrs/ v. ★★ verso *The first three verses are about her childhood.*

version /'vɜrʒ(ə)n/ n. ★★★ versão *This is the new version of the video game.*

very /'veri/ adj. adv. ★★★ muito *This movie is very interesting.*

veterinarian /ˌvet(ə)rɪ'neriən/ n. veterinário *Nancy is a veterinarian because she likes to take care of animals.*

victorious /vɪk'tɔriəs/ adj. vitorioso *The award represented the confirmation of a victorious journey.*

view /vju/ n. vista, visita, visualização *My blog had 7 views this week.*

viral /'vaɪrəl/ adj. viral, rapidamente popularizado *Within weeks, her blog went viral.*

visionary /'vɪʒ(ə)nˌeri/ adj. visionário *Their success owes a lot to his visionary leadership.*

visit /'vɪzɪt/ v. ★★★ visitar *Carina visits her grandparents every weekend.* **visitor** visitante

vocabulary /voʊ'kæbjəˌleri/ n. ★ vocabulário *Let's learn some words and improve our vocabulary.*

W

wait /weɪt/ v. ★★★ esperar *Wait a minute, please.*

walk /wɔk/ v. ★★★ andar *Walking is one of my favorite hobbies.*

want /wɑnt/ v. ★★★ querer *I want to travel to China.*

wanted /'wɑntəd/ adj. ★ procurado *He is wanted for murder.*

war /wɔr/ n. ★★★ guerra *World War II ended in 1945.*

was /wɑz/ v. past of be *Ivan was my teacher in the 1990s.*

washing machine n. ★ máquina de lavar *The washing machine is not working. You will have to wash your clothes by hand.*

waste /weɪst/ n. ★★★ desperdício *Staying here is a waste of time.*

watch /wɑtʃ/ v. ★★★ ver, assistir *Dorothy and Ron watch TV only on the weekends.*

waterslide /'wɔtərˌslaɪd/ n. tobogã *We played on waterslide in the theme park.*

watermelon /'wɔtərˌmelən/ n. melancia *Watermelon juice is quite popular in Brazil.*

way /weɪ/ n. ★★★ caminho, via *This way is shorter than through the main road.*

week /wik/ n. ★★★ semana *A week is composed of seven days.*

weekend /'wikˌend/ n. ★★★ fim de semana *The bus service is free on weekends.*

weigh /weɪ/ v. ★★ pesar *Tell me Clare, how much do you weigh?*

weight /weɪt/ n. ★★★ peso *We use kilos and grams as a measure of weight.*

what /wɑt/ adv. det. predet. inter. pron. ★★★ o que *What is your name?*

whatever /wɑt'evər/ adv. conj. pron. ★★★ o que quer que *Now you are free to do whatever you want.*

when /wen/ adv. conj. ★★★ quando *When is your birthday?*

wheather /'weðər/ n. ★★★ clima *Employees are deciding whether to accept the offer.*

which /wɪtʃ/ deter. ★★★ qual *Which cap do you prefer?*

while /waɪl/ conj. ★★★ enquanto *Listen to this song while I have a shower.*

who /hu/ pron. ★★★ quem *Who is your favorite singer?*

whole /hoʊl/ n. ★★★ completo, inteiro *Two halves make a whole.*

why /waɪ/ adv. ★★★ por que *Why do dogs bark?*

will /wɪl/ modal (indicador de futuro) *There will be a short ceremony at the war memorial.*

will /wɪl/ n. desejo *If this is your will, then do it.*

winter /'wɪntər/ n. ★★★ inverno *We spend the winter in the south.*

wire /waɪr/ n. ★★ fio *The sticks were tied in bundles with wire.*

wise /waɪz/ adj. ★★ sábio *I don't think it's wise to teachyour children at home.*

wish /wɪʃ/ v. n. ★★★ desejar; desejo *I wish you a Merry Christmas and a Happy New Year.*

without /wɪð'aʊt/ adv. prep. ★★★ sem *Do not leave without your jacket; it's raining.*

wool /wʊl/ n. ★★ lã *This coat is made of wool.*

word /wɜrd/ n. ★★★ palavra *I is a very short word.*

work /wɜrk/ v. n. ★★★ trabalhar; trabalho *Flight attendants might work up to 18 hours a day.*

world /wɜrld/ n. ★★★ mundo *There are endless living creatures in our world.*

worry /'wʌri/ v. ★★★ preocupar-se *Don't worry about the exams, you'll be fine.*

worship /'wɜrˌʃɪp/ v. ★ adorar (religiosamente) *The building has been a place of worship since the eighth century.*

would /wʊd/ mod. v. ★★★ gostaria *I would like a glass of water.*

wrap /ræp/ v. ★★ enrolar *Please wrap the present in nice paper.*

wristband /'rɪstˌbænd/ n. pulseira de plástico *Wristbands became a fad in the 2000s.*

write /raɪt/ v. ★★★ escrever *I always write emails to my friends.* **writing** redação

writer /'raɪtər/ n. ★★★ escritor *Paulo Coelho is a Brazilian writer who's famous worldwide.*

wrong /rɔŋ/ adj. ★★★ errado *What is not correct is wrong.*

X

xenophobia /ˌzinə'foʊbiə/ n. xenofobia *Xenophobia is a stupid prejudice against foreigners.*

Y

year /jɪr/ n. ★★★ ano *This is the year of 2014.*

yesterday /'jestərˌdeɪ/ adv. ★★★ ontem *Yesterday was my sister's birthday.*

yolk /joʊk/ n. gema de ovo *We do not use yolks to make this dessert.*

young /jʌŋ/ adj. ★★★ jovem *My cousin is really young; he is 17 years old.*

youth /juθ/ n. ★★★ juventude *This club is a kind of youth association.*

Website references

Page 15 **TripAdvisor.com** <www.tripadvisor.com>. Accessed August 2011.

Page 21 **InfoPlease.com** <www.infoplease.com/world/statistics/school-years.html>. Accessed August 2011.

Page 23 **TripAdvisor.com** <www.tripadvisor.com>. Accessed August 2011.

Page 28 **Memecentral.com** <www.memecentral.com/>. Accessed February 2012.
Truthy.Indiana.edu <http://truthy.indiana.edu/faq>. Accessed February 2012.
Memetics.TimTyler.org <http://memetics.timtyler.org/faq/>. Accessed February 2012.

Page 33 **Neok12.com** <www.neok12.com/php/watch.php?v=zX57774078797d7564675a0a&t=Genetics>. Accessed February 2012.
Home.EarthLink.net <Home.EarthLink.net>. Accessed April 2012.

Page 35 **GlassGiant.com** <glassgiant.com>. Accessed April 2012.

Page 39 **The Guardian** <www.guardian.co.uk>. Accessed April 2012.

Page 44 **TheOriens.com** <http://theoriens.com>. Accessed February 2012.

Page 49 **UN.org** <http://pt.wikipedia.org/wiki/Stokely_Carmichael>. Accessed January 2012.

Page 57 **BrazzilMag.com** <www.brazzilmag.com/news>. Accessed February 2012.

Page 64 **TimesOnline.co.uk** <www.timesonline.co.uk/tol/life_and_style/ food_and_drink/article5627478.ece>. Accessed February 2012.

Page 65 **ChooseMyPlate.gov** <www.choosemyplate.gov>. Accessed February 2012.

Page 68 **Amazon.com** <www.amazon.com>. Accessed March 2012.

Page 70 **PlanetGreen.Discovery.com** <www.planetgreen.discovery.com>. Accessed February 2012.

Page 72 **TripAdvisor.com** <www.tripadvisor.com/hotels>. Accessed April 2012.
Iesonava.info <www.iesonava.info/olgaenlared/edpronunciation.htm>. Accessed April 2012.
EduTube.org <www.edutube.org/video/what-causes-different-seasons-animation>. Accessed April 2012.
Neok12.com <www.neok12.com/php/watch.php?v=zX57774078797d7564675a0a&t=Genetics>. Accessed February 2012.

Page 73 **Osocio.org** <http://osocio.org/category/discrimination/>. Accessed April 2012.
UN.org <www.un.org/en/documents/udhr/>. Accessed February 2012.
DiscoveryChannel.ca <http://watch.discoverychannel.ca/how-its-made/#clip371234>. Accessed February 2012.
Anvisa.gov.br <www.anvisa.gov.br/legis/resol/12_78_biscoitos>. Accessed April 2012 .
MacMillanDictionary.com <www.macmillandictionary.com/thesaurus-category/british/words-used-to-describe-the-state-or-consistency-of-food>. Accessed April 2012.
SoundofEnglish.org <www.soundsofenglish.org/pronunciation/index>. Accessed February 2012.

Page 79 **Articles.LATimes.com** <articles.latimes.com/2004/jun/24/local/me-mattie24>. Accessed August 2011.

Page 82 **Libras.org** <www.libras.org.br/libras.php>. Accessed April 2012.

Page 91 **WJBF.com** <www2.wjbf.com/news/2011/sep/07/2/peta-protest-52832-vi-102218/>. Accessed April 2012.
News.stv.tv <http://news.stv.tv/scotland/268941-130-rise-in-stray-dogs-put-down-by-local-authorities/>. Accessed April 2012.
DailyTimes.com.pk <www.dailytimes.com.pk/default.asp?page=2011%5C09%5C09%5Cstory_9-9-2011_pg9_3>. Accessed April 2012.
GlobeGazette.com <http://globegazette.com/news/local/humane-society-takes-in-dogs-from-puppy-mill/article_e2d7edf4-e086-11e0-871e-001cc4c002e0.html#ixzz1YQlQJjaH>. Accessed April 2012.
WRDW.com <www.wrdw.com/health/headlines/Disabled_woman_awarded_free_service_dog_in_Augusta_129903468.html>. Accessed April 2012.
WCTV.tv <www.wctv.tv/news/headlines/Florida_Introduces_Bill_to_Ban_Farm_Animal_Confinement_117821523.html?ref=523>. Accessed April 2012.

Page 96 **Parade.com** <www.parade.com/pets/articles/090111-dog-whisperer.html>. Accessed April 2012.

Page 104 **Camara.sp.gov.br** <www.camara.sp.gov.br>. Accessed April 2012.

Page 116 **MamaDragonfly2677.hubpages.com** <mamadragonfly2677.hubpages.com/hub/easter-island-and-lessons-learned>. Accessed April 2012.

Page 136 **IMDB.com** <www.imdb.com/title/tt0204824/>. Accessed April 2012.

Page 137 **QuotationsPage.com** <www.quotationspage.com/>. Accessed April 2012.
RightBrainTerrain.com <http://rightbrainterrain.com/manifesto.htm>. Accessed April 2012.

Bibliography

BAKHTIN, M.; VOLOCHINOV, V. N. *Marxismo e filosofia da linguagem*. 11. ed. São Paulo: Hucitec, 2004.

BAWARSHI, A.; DEVITT, A.; REIFF, M. J. *Scenes of Writing: Strategies for Composing with Genres*. New York: Pearson Longman, 2004.

BAZERMAN, C. *Gêneros textuais, tipificação e interação*. São Paulo: Cortez, 2005.

BRASIL. Secretaria de Educação Fundamental. *Parâmetros curriculares nacionais: terceiro e quarto ciclos do Ensino Fundamental: língua estrangeira moderna*. Brasília: MEC, 1998.

BROWN, H. D. Teaching by Principles: *An Interactive Approach to Language Pedagogy*. New York: Pearson, 2001.

COSCARELLI, V. C.; RIBEIRO, A. E. *Letramento digital: aspectos sociais e possibilidades pedagógicas*. Belo Horizonte: Ceale / Autêntica, 2007.

FREIRE, P. *Pedagogia da autonomia: saberes necessários à prática educativa*. São Paulo: Paz e Terra, 1996.

GOWER, R.; PHILLIPS, D.; WALTERS, S. *Teaching Practice. A Handbook for Teachers in Training*. Oxford: Macmillan, 1995.

HARMER, J. *How to Teach English: An Introduction to the Practice of English Language Teaching*. Harlow: Pearson Longman, 2007.

HERNANDEZ, F.; VENTURA, M. *Organização do Currículo por Projetos de Trabalho. O Conhecimento e um Caleidoscópio*. Porto Alegre: Artmed, 1998

JOHNSON, K.; MORROW, K. *Communication in the Classroom*. Harlow: Pearson, 1990.

KLEIMAN, A. B.; MORAES, S. E. *Leitura e interdisciplinaridade: tecendo redes nos projetos da escola*. Campinas: Mercado de Letras, 1999.

KRESS, Gunther. *Reading Images: Multimodality, Representation and New Media*. Disponível em: <www.knowledgepresentation.org/BuildingTheFuture/Kress2/Kress2.html>. Acesso em: 12 dez. 2006.

MEHISTO, P.; MARSH, D.; FRIGOLS, M. J. *Uncovering CLIL: Content and Language Integrated Learning in Bilingual and Multilingual Education*. Oxford: Macmillan, 2008.

MEURER, J. L.; BONINI, A.; MOTTA-ROTH, D. (Org.). *Gêneros: teorias, métodos, debates*. São Paulo: Parábola Editorial, 2005.

NUNAN, D. *Task-Based Language Teaching*. Cambridge: CUP, 2004.

RAJAGOPALAN, K. *Por uma linguística crítica: linguagem, identidade e a questão ética*. São Paulo: Parábola Editorial, 2003.

SCHNEUWLY, B.; DOLZ, J.; HALLER, S. *Gêneros orais e escritos na escola*. Trad. e org. ROJO, R. H. R.; CORDEIRO, G. S. Campinas: Mercado de Letras, 2004.

SCRIVENER, J. *Learning Teaching*. Oxford: Macmillan, 2004.

SIGNORINI, I.; CAVALCANTI, M. C. (Org.). *Linguística aplicada e transdisciplinaridade*. Campinas: Mercado de Letras, 2004.

TANNER, R.; GREEN C. *Tasks for Teacher Education: A Reference Approach Coursebook*. Harlow: Longman, 1998.

THORNBURY, S.; SLADE, D. *Conversation: From Description to Pedagogy*. Cambridge: CUP, 2006.

UR, P. *A Course in Language Teaching: Practice and theory*. Cambridge: CUP, 2001.

When and how to use your DVD-ROM

Multimedia Content 1 – My weekend	
When to use	After *Speaking*, page 20 (Unit 1)
Content	Game about a teenager's weekend
Purpose	To practice the Simple Past of verbs in context.
What to do	Match the pictures with the texts they describe.
Tips	Observe the pictures and think of verbs that will probably be used to describe the scene.
Multimedia Content 2 – Carnivals around the world	
When to use	After *Crossroads*, page 21 (Unit 1)
Content	Infographics about Carnival
Purpose	To inform about Carnival celebrations around the world.
What to do	Read and learn more about Carnival festivities around the world.
Tips	Pay attention to similarities and differences among different Carnival celebrations around the world.
Multimedia Content 3 – A timeline of haircuts	
When to use	After *Vocabulary* , page 32 (Unit 2)
Content	Infographics about the evolution of hairstyles
Purpose	To inform about hairstyles in fashion in certain periods of modern history.
What to do	Read the descriptions and observe the pictures.
Tips	Pay attention to the words used to describe each hairstyle.
Multimedia Content 4 – Genetics	
When to use	After *Crossroads*, page 33 (Unit 2)
Content	Simulator of the chromosome combination responsible for determining the gender of an embryo
Purpose	To expand the topic "genetics" seen in *Crossroads*.
What to do	Combine the different chromosomes and see how the gender of an embryo is determined.
Tips	Think of other human characteristics that may be determined by genes. Talk to your science teacher, research in the school library or on the Internet, and confirm your assumptions.
Multimedia Content 5 – The danger of stereotypes	
When to use	After *Vocabulary*, page 46 (Unit 3)
Content	Game about stereotypes
Purpose	To think of how stereotypes may lead to prejudice and segregation.
What to do	Drag to the garbage can all sentences that mention some kind of stereotype.
Tips	Think about how stereotypes and subjective interpretations may disturb our communication and the way we perceive other people.

Multimedia Content 6 – Hot dogs	
When to use	Before *Crossroads*, page 64 (Unit 4)
Content	Infographics about hot dogs
Purpose	To introduce the history of the hot dog, how it is made, and curiosities about it.
What to do	Read the information carefully and learn more about hot dogs.
Tips	Write down what you would like to have more information about.

Multimedia Content 7 – Sign language	
When to use	After *Crossroads*, page 82 (Unit 5)
Content	Video with some sentences in LIBRAS
Purpose	To teach some basic expressions in sign language.
What to do	Observe the signs carefully and repeat them.
Tips	Think of the logic behind each sign. For example: the sign for "good morning" represents the sun rising.

Multimedia Content 8 – Responsible dog owners	
When to use	Before *Listening*, page 96 (Unit 6)
Content	Quiz about how to be a responsible dog owner
Purpose	To test knowledge about what a responsible dog owner does.
What to do	Answer the questions honestly and analyze your results.
Tips	Think about what you can do to improve not only your attitudes but also other people's attitudes concerning responsible treatment of pets.

Multimedia Content 9 – The future	
When to use	After *Pronunciation*, page 111 (Unit 7)
Content	Game about future predictions
Purpose	To introduce adequate vocabulary to make predictions; practice the grammar structure of the unit.
What to do	Read the predictions, and then click on "agree" or "disagree." See your results, and check whether your predictions are aligned with a famous scientist's predictions.
Tips	If necessary, look in a dictionary before giving opinions.

Multimedia Content 10 – Accents	
When to use	After *Pronunciation*, page 123 (Unit 8)
Content	Video with TV news about accents
Purpose	To test your listening skills with an authentic video.
What to do	Watch the video and answer the questions that follow.
Tips	Do not bother understanding all words in all sentences. Focus on the words you understand. Use logic and common sense to understand the main ideas in the news.

Capa: **Getty Images:** Frank Slack /Getty Images (Cidade do Cabo) Michael Hanson/Getty Images (Machu Picchu) David Malan /Getty Images (fotos)

© 2011 Mattie J.T. Stepanek and Jennifer Smith Stepanek: 102 (Mattie)

© Sony Corporation: 45

© DreamWorks Animation SKG: 31 (Poster-how-to-train-your-dragon)

© Félix Nadar: 133

© Juvenal Pereira: 104

© The Floating Press: 132

choosemyplate.gov: 64 (tabela)

Coleção Particular: 25, 28, 35

Courtesy of the Archives, Philip Weltner Library, Oglethorpe University: 40 (Crypt of Civilization)

Folhapress: Maria do Carmo 63 (tucupi)

Leons Story © Farrar, Straus and Giroux: 68 (Leon)

Modernistas 1922, ed. Alumbramento: 128

Heelys Worldwide: 32, 37 (tênis com rodinhas)

www.CartoonStock.com: 42, 43 (cartum cachorros), 42, 44 (cartum arca), 42, 45 (cartum homem)

Gabriella Fabbri: 133

www.discriminatie.nl: 45 (poster 1, 2 e 3)

Getty Images: Chris Walter/Wireimages 38 (Journey), Image Source 125,Liam Norris 54 (mesa), Time & Life Pictures 75 (tamagochi), Javier Pierini 107,Leigh Vogel 90 (1e), photosindia 106,Thomas Jackson 76, 77

Shutterstock: Alexander Chaikin 116 (2b), Alexander Raths 113 (cientistas), AlexTois 62 (kiwi), alphaspirit 24 (computador), Amanda Clements 62 (abacaxi), AnetaPics 96 (beagle), Archipoch 62 (banana), ARENA Creative 54 (geladeira), 86 (treinador), ArtmannWitte 138 (d), auremar 112 (d), BestPhotoStudio 124 (d), Björn Erlandsson 95 Blend Images 124 (a), Boris Djuranovic 90 (1d), Brenda Carson 41 (caixa), casadaphoto 18 (cidade), Catalin Petolea 31 (no computador), Chris Harvey 37 (fantasiado), Christian Delbert 102 (caderno), Christopher Parypa 18 (caranguejo), CLIPAREA l Custom media 108 (corpo humano), Coprid 58 (cream cracker), CREATISTA 93 (menino), Daniel Korzeniewski 138 (c), Darren Baker 85 (1), David Ewing Photography 120 (3a), David Fowler 109 dean bertoncelj 110 (2), Diego Cervo 86 (casal 1), Dmitriy Shironosov 139 (4), dragon_fang 110 (3), ejwhite 30 (vendo TV), Elena Elisseeva 85 (2c), 112 (a), Eric Isselée 92 ExaMedia Photography 37 (SD card), Golden Pixels LLC 111 (e), Goodluz 138 (b), 139 (3d), Gregory Albertini 96 (gato), gualtiero boffi 108 (aspirador), Hamik 12, 13 (abertura), Helder Almeida 29 (meninos), ilFede 111 (b), Indigo Fish 14 (menino dirigindo), InnervisionArt 96 (macaco), iofoto 37 (moicano), Jaimie Duplass 58 (crispy), Jane September 111 (d), Joe Seer 93 (Cesar Millan), Jose Gil 83 karnizz 14 (parque aquático), Konstantin Karchevskiy 90 (1f), langdu 62 (jaca), Lars Christensen 96 (cão-guia), 37 (sudoku), Leah-Anne Thompson 32 (garota), Len Green 32 (óculos), Lisa S. 112 (c), Losevsky Pavel 85 (2d), marcokenya 88, 89 Martin Lehmann 37 (stand up comedy), MartiniDry 124 (b), Michael Pettigrew 96 (cão e gato), Mino Surkala 32 (SD card), MNStudio 139 (3e), Monkey Business Images 121 Muellek Josef 90 (1b), Nadezda Boltaca 66 (dado e peças), Natali Glado 94 nito 58 (gelatina), Oleg Golovnev 62 (melancia), Olga Besnard 48 (passeata), ostill 16 (praia), OtnaYdur 86 (casal 2), Pablo Scapinachis 70 (divisão), Petrenko Andriy 127 Phase4Photography 37 (japonesa), Philip Lange 36 (Shopping Dubai), PhotoSky 4t com 120 (3b), Pinkcandy 112 (b), R. Gino Santa Maria 108 (TV), Rene Jansa 139 (3b), Roberto Sanchez 32 (sudoku), Roman Sinichkin 138 (a), Scorpp 90 (1a), Scott T Slattery 93 (porquinhos), Sebastian Kaulitzki 33 (DNA), Simone Voigt 60 (sanduíche), slava296 14 (piscina), Smirnof 37 (calça apertada), sniegirova mariia 120 (2), stefanolunardi 111 (c), Stephen VanHorn 139 (3a), Straight 8 Photography 113 (tanque), Supri Suharjoto 124 (c), szefei 116 (2a), tan4ikk 41 (ícones), terekhov igor 138 (f), testing 32 (japonesa), Tomas Sereda 90 (1c), Tomaz Kunst 116 (moais), Ulrich Mueller 96 (porco), Varina and Jay Patel 46 (pés), Vasily Smirnov 138 (e), Vitaly Titov & Maria Sidelnikova 96 (cão com roupa), Vladimir Mucibabic 81 Vladislav Gurfinkel 58 (dry), Voronin76 108 (fax), vvoe 14 (cama), wavebreakmedia ltd 139 (3c), Shutterstock 31 (fazenda), 56 (bolacha 1), 56 (bolacha 2), 56 (bolacha 3), 56 (bolacha 4), 56 (bolacha 5), 56 (bolacha 6), 56 (bolacha 7), 57 (bolacha recheada), 58 (gomas), 58 (granulado), 58 (crumbly), 58 (batatinhas), 59 (escoteira), 62 (romã), 63 (vatapá), 64 (jamie oliver), 75 (terrário), 75 (bambolê), 72, 73 (looking back 1), 72, 74 (looking back 2)

SXC: dcubillas 46 (religiões 4), Dr_Evil 46 (religiões 3), Kashfia Rahman 46 (religiões 1), normatta 17 (cenário), Patricia Dekker / SXC 15 (laptop), Philippe Ramakers 46 (senhora), ramzi hashisho 46 (religiões 2), Renaude Hatsedakis / sxc 15 (paraquedas), Rob Owen-Wahl/SXC 15 (foto)

Thinkstock: AbleStock.com 75 (calça), Alexia Khruscheva 16 (cavalo), BananaStock 34 (patinetes), 71 (feira), 85 (2a), Brand X Pictures 16 (amigos), 85 (2g), Comstock 16 (hiking), 16 (sala), 51 (computador), 75 (bota), Creatas 20 (menina), 22 (grupo), 50 (mãe e filho), 52 (casal jovem), 56 (aveia), 85 (2f), Digital Video 32 (adolescente), Digital Vision 29 (grupo de amigos), 14 (hotel), 19 (amigos), 20 (carro), 34 (sala), 34 (3 meninas), Hemera 21 (rotação), 71 (bananeira), 75 (pingente), 100 (bezerro, cavalo, porco, cordeiro, pintinho), iStockphoto 16 (shopping), 16 (mergulho), 31 (pulseira), 32 (cabelo), 34 (tipoia), 52 (adulto e criança), 56 (farinha), 56 (cacau), 56 (bicarbonato), 63 (quindim), 85 (2b), 85 (2e), Lifesize 52 (senhor), Liquidlibrary 50 (prova), Lisa F. Young 85 (2h), Photodisc 32 (stand up comedy), 74 (na cozinha), iStockphoto 82 100 (pato), Photodisc 120 (3c)

O **Macmillan Dictionary** foi usado como referência na produção do *Minidictionary*.

Agradecimentos

Gostaríamos de expressar nossos agradecimentos às pessoas que nos acompanharam ao longo desta jornada:

- às nossas famílias, pela compreensão e apoio incondicional, sem julgamentos ou críticas quanto às nossas escolhas profissionais;
- a todos os professores que passaram por nossas vidas e que inspiraram essa experiência magnífica de compartilhar conhecimentos;
- aos nossos amigos e colegas de trabalho, que nos proporcionaram aprendizados valiosos e conforto nos momentos difíceis da carreira;
- a todos os alunos, razão de nossa existência, por terem mantido acesa a chama do entusiasmo, dedicação e amor pelo ensino;
- e também a você, usuário deste livro. Desejamos que você tenha uma carreira tão gratificante e apaixonante quanto as nossas.

Obrigado!

Os autores.